Endorsements

"On my shelf full of AT books, among the countless linear narratives, tales, and wondrous hiking experiences, Wehrwein's book stands alone--a singular, shimmering emerald, exposing a heroic healing quest amidst the grandeur, beauty, and deeply loving care of Nature. Elegantly weaving the inner and the outer, this swirling, poetic encapsulation reveals the powerful healing available for us when we *listen*, when the loving forces of Nature become audible to our souls, and we once again find our salvation." - J.David Forbes, M.D.

"Starting, like Dante, in the darkness of midlife despair, the author (not a trained poet) discovers by serendipitous grace how to survive and eventually heal from the deadly shame that has followed him since his childhood and youth on account of multiple sexual assaults. His transformative way leads him over the whole, long Appalachian Trail. It requires him to take in stride whatever fate deals out, whether deadly dangers or the gifts of ancient spirits and fellow hikers. He is sustained above all by the spirit of Crow and his beloved's serene, redeeming presence. These poems, written in the first person and the present tense, are so personal that a reader enters the life of Gary (Crow Feathah) as a friend. Meanwhile, invited or not, death hovers everywhere. On a first hike in winter, paralyzed by inner agony, Gary barely escapes a half-intended suicide. During the depths of the Covid pandemic, he confronts the real risk that he will 'die in Denia.' The earned ending of the epic reads: 'I live alive in mystery! For that, there is no death penalty!'" -Ann Conrad Lammers, Ph.D.

"I am witness to your journey told in stories on the trail, experienced together along the trail, and shared again as the trail continues to lead me with you as my witness. The bond that is walking the trail has opened to healing, and keen witness to other's wounds, attention to our own wounds, and healing within a community of sharing is dynamic in the written record of your epoch. The white blazes of your AT experience invite my own memories, and the blue blaze side trails enhance the tales told on the trail. I witnessed your journey blessed by crow feathers on the path as you witnessed the pace of my journey while the thunder was laughing. Thank you for bringing this epoch poem to life on the printed page for others to find a voice for healing on their passage through life-changing wounds and daily healing events." Denis T Noonan III, D.Min., Licensed Pastoral Counselor, Aka: Laughin Thundah

"Gary is a consummate Cartographer of the Soul. In his poetry, he weaves his experiences of suffering and healing, hiking the Appalachian Trail, Jungian psychology, and faith. All these come together in a challenging and accessible narrative that invites readers to journey into their own soul."--Leonard Fleischer, Ed., Retired Clinical Psychologist, Professor Emeritus, Keene State College.

"It is said that nobody gets out of childhood without psychic and emotional wounds. Gary Wehrwein, bravely and unflinchingly, negotiates that difficult psychic and emotional terrain in Hike to Alive. In this vivid story, told as an epic poem, Wehrwein shows that there is a way to transform the debilitating effects of childhood trauma. On a life-changing journey in the prism of wild nature, the reader can feel the turmoil and the potential of encountering their own inner wilderness. In a series of poems written over years of hiking the Appalachian Trail, we can encounter the immediacy and intensity of the author's emotional evolution through those challenges. There is a sense of liberation, of coming out of the shadows and living into a vital and meaningful life. "Hike to Alive" points the way." -Len Fleischer, Ed.D., Retired Clinical Psychologist Professor Emeritus

"Internal Family systems practitioners refer to Trail Heads as the entry points into the wilderness places of the inner world. The line between the inner and outer spaces is often quite thin, a kind of liminal space. Accompany Gary Wehrwein as he steps onto the Appalachian Trail, which becomes a trailhead into his inner world and the healing of sexual trauma. Walk with him from the Knife's Edge led by a crow feather into that time and space in between wherein lives pain, mystery, magic, rage, tears, laughter, love, and the impetus toward healing, a space of grit and grace, courage and fear and finally, a peace that baths you in joy and solidarity and perhaps a taste of your own healing."-William F. Beardslee, M.Div., Pastor, Pastoral Psychotherapist

HIKE TO ALIVE

Hike to Alive

An Epic Poem from Trauma to Transformation

Gary E. Wehrwein

SANTOS BOOKS
EVERY STORY SACRED

Contents

To Denis T. Noonan III, D.Min.
Aka Laughin Thundah
Who invited me to
section-hike the Appalachian Trail.

"Laughin Thundah" is "Brother," Friend, witness
to my experience of
Life, Death, Life Transformation
As we prepare for timeless life.
See you "now" and "later."
Love, Feathah

Preface

When I was three, my father lifted me to his bedroom window to see sturgeon jump through a full moon reflection on the Kennebec River. In the middle of that night, a seed of great mystery became real in my psyche.

In 1992, section hiking the Appalachian Trail began to grow this unconscious, liminal seed to consciousness and eventually greater personal wholeness.

Along the way, I was helped by childhood church-going, High school English teacher, Mrs. Withey, Norwich University, Andover Newton Theological Seminary, discovery of psychology, pastoral psychotherapy, counseling, hospice chaplaincy, and through serving two rural pastorates. All these contribute to the cultivation and weeding of my spiritual path.

That early seed-planting life continues to grow today as I walk my soul path on and off the AT.

My first choir director told me, "Gary, your mind is all over the place in how poems express metaphor and symbol as they lead to deeper spiritual paths."

A sequential enumeration is not the way it was. To the reader, these poems written here may "feel" disorderly and lack clear form. Frankly, these poems are not written mile after mile, page after page.

I didn't intend them to be written sequentially. The reader may feel an absence of "left out" geographical features or expected symbolism. These poems come from the moon's reflection on the river where God spawns a sturgeon seed. When liminal space and sturgeon seed combine, "known and unknown," hearing and seeing bring mystery alive.

On the Appalachian Trail comes Crow. I discovered a "certain" symbolic healing reality I never knew existed. From 1992-2001, my midlife journey connected "known and unknown" with Crow. Who enabled me then and now to "redefine, reorient, restore, heal" my life and keep on growing it to greater wholeness.

My reality is both here and there, be it earthy and profane or glorious and full of healing grace. God's space in the full moon reflection became shared space when Dad lifted me to the window to see what he saw. For whatever reason, God and Dad connected and brought my very young soul into a great Mystery!

This Epic is an invitation for readers at any state or stage in life to put on hiking boots or bare feet. Accept the invitation. Get on the trail and hike! Become conscious to become whole. Let the "Trail" walk you!

It's never too late to "hike" toward wholeness, whatever wholeness is for you.

Let Mother Nature sit you on a stump or river bank amidst a bed of trillium or daylilies. Listen to Crow give you an opportunity to heal.

---Gary Wehrwein, Keene, New Hampshire

PART I: THE MYSTERY OF LIFE AND DEATH

1

Prologue

All Saint's Day--Halloween 1981
T'was All Hallows Eve
when fires are lit,
costumes worn,
black cats yowl and spit,
call out evil spirits,
dance dusk to dawn.

Back in 1981
Hiking buddy, Thom
without telling "why,"
invites me from bed early to rise,
climb Mt. Washington
into fierce cloudy grey realms
of ghosts and goblins
on that always remembered
fateful day.

"Saint" Thom
saw what I did not, could not see:
my life is an ugly mess,
living in a black cloud,

recently divorced,
situationally depressed.

We string up our boots
at Cog Railway Station.
Lock up, leave behind
old orange, VW pumpkin.

It's Shadow Time!
Time to lay bare,
take off the mask,
unbox anger, resentment, sorrow, fear,
let go of gripping monsters,
hike into realms of seen, unseen uncertainties,
expose hidden inner identities.

The holy, unholy weather stew plot thickens.
Evil spirits, not sun, season weather soup.
Thick dark, light threatening clouds,
heavy hurts, grief, pain simmer.
Ghost faces, dragon's teeth ferment,
boil down, harkening, darkening
soul laden shame.

Thom guides into high mountain dangers.
Going "up" feels like
Virgil taking Dante "down"
into hot fires of living hell.
First, I'm hot, then I'm not.
Firey darkness, suicidal fantasies
raise pot's top.

My soul is in shambles.
The Devil invites me to dance.
I accept its seductive invitation.
What a good time for an accident!
Icy ledges would do the trick.
I can slip, slide, dance over that
life-death edge really quick!
Halloween is a good day for
for such an "accidental" trick.

A friend did that.
He never came back!
No one would care. Do I dare
to "dance" freeze myself in ice
instead of burn in fire?

Ghostly witches, dragon voices
whirl round in my head
whisper: "Do it…. Do it….
You won't even know you're dead!
Make the choice!"

I'm brought low by awful cold.
"You are entering
Worst Weather in the World,"
a barely visible sign says.
My mind says:
"Wind, Cold, Ice, Snow
take my body, make it ice.
I'm not worth at any price
another day in paradise!
Roll the dice!"

A Shadow appears
through thick icy mist:
Lake of the Clouds Hut.

I hear Thom's voice:
"We must turn around!
We must go down now!"

His words thaw, untie the Gordian Knot
of frozen emotion, thought, confusion,
bound up frightful suicidal delusion.

Terrified, relieved I turn around.
Ice needles by the thousands
sting my face.
Eyes are squinty, like seeing through a veil.

I slip. Fall hard.
Tumble down steep icy edges.
Out of deep nowhere inside, I hear:
"I don't want to die sliding off ledges,
today or any day. This I pledge."

God spoke through Thom.
No harshness, no demeaning roar:
"Kick over the pot!
We must turn around!
We must go down!"

Firm strength, compassion
caring from Thom
turns me around.

Ice crystals melt to tears,
stream down
like Amanoosuc streams down
Big "W's" face.

We enter the orange VW pumpkin.
Leave Cog Railway parking lot vacant, empty.
Rolling down the road into N. Conway,
I see little feet carry on their heads
white bone skulls, Cinderellas,

ghosts, goblins, monsters, witches
through N. Conway streets.
From Thom's fiery cheeks,
his rosy red face glows.
To get soup and a sandwitch we go.
Filled with Gratitude
a life-saving debt
to "Saint" Thom, I'll always owe.

2

If I Die in Denia

I.
If I die in Denia, don't bury me there.
Take my ashes to New Hampshire.
Float them in White Mountain air.

Scatter some on Mt. Katahdin
for there this story begins.
Leave a few on the Appalachian Trail,
which leads to telling this life-changing tale.

Don't forget the Kennebec!
Toss a few on the river:
I saw Sturgeon jump through the moon,
that night Dad held me to the window.

II.
In late night sky
A few stars lingered
showering hope
that would determine whether
I live or die.

I take that first step,
leave safety
of Chimney Pond shelter.
Cross the threshold,
plant feet solid
on unfamiliar ground.

Up Dudley Trail toward Pamola peak,
I climb through the giant boulder field,
to seek new meaning for my confused,
wounded, midlife mind.

I reach the Peak
in clear blue late-night dawn.
There blurry, curious beauty
of light and dark is born.
I'm anxious, alone,
atop Katahdin's summit.
No one else in sight
except Venus fading
in early morning light.

My old green external frame pack
is heavy with pain's
agony of confused depression.
A deep sense of long held unworthy obsession,
hangs hard on my shoulders and back.

The load freezes me in time.
This must be the way Abraham felt
taking Isaac to Mt. Moriah's summit of sacrifice
along his terrifying rocky road.

Uncertain opposites rage inside.
I stand exposed, vulnerable, no place to hide.
I feel God's absence, mine besides.
Yet remember, from Genesis
"On the mountain God will provide."

In emerging blue-gray early light,
I stand fearful, isolated, alone,
barren without,
time-frozen within.

III.
"Pamola" is wandering Bird Spirit
with human body,
head of a moose,
eagle wings and feet.
I would need these "extras"
to guide me to Baxter Peak.

Moved by "Bird Spirit,"
My outer eyes wander to the Peak.
My inner eyes notice unfamiliar stirrings
set in motion by shaky feet.
Hiking 2,190 miles from Maine to Georgia
to search for my life's Tree
could give Life new meaning for me!

"What's the worth! What's the worth!
I can't say.
I can't say because I feel worthless
even to search for worthiness.

I must draw on God's promise:

"On the mountain Yahweh provides"
this dawning day and every day.

Eighty miles away, Mother Nature has her say
as Poseidon bursts from the Atlantic,
on eastern horizon of the USA.
Sun's first light spreads like feathers,
shining behind Mt Desert
beginning its arching journey,
and mine, this glorious new day!

3

Chimney

Energized by morning's first light,
I adjust my old green pack.
Up Knife Edge I gaze to Baxter Peak.
I cross another threshold,
take first steps very steep,
follow cairns along Katahdin's spiny back.

My body shivers.
My legs quiver.
No other hiker do I see.

In early light
Those injected, introjected fears,
awaken primitive notions of Death and Life,
nag at the ground of my very being.
A pedophiliac,
trashed my sense of trust.
Agoraphobic tendencies steal my breath,
yell out "Hell no! I won't go!"
Fears bring me to tears.

At chimney's edge I turn,
see far behind me,
a human figure,
small as an ant.

Before me, an empty black circle
reveals the chimney door
to Life's silent unconscious dimension.
I'll need more than a long-handled broom
to sweep profound vulnerability
from these steep rocky walls!
They wait for my risk
to be swallowed into the abyss
the way the whale swallowed Jonah.

Beyond the black hole,
I look across darkness.
Cairns point toward Baxter peak.
They speak of Life and death swirling within.
I wonder:
Will this descent into earth be my tomb?
Will ascent heal,
cause my life to bloom?

I drop into the abyss.
My face against the cliff.
Foot over foot, hand over hand
I slip into unknown depths.
My heart beats hard and fast.
I fear death. Cling dearly to life,
as breath rhythms guide entry
to find new ground of my being.

Painted gold by rays,
of Sun's "new day" light,
rocky cairns ahead invite.
With fear softened, strength renewed,
the sharp, narrow Knife Edge,
like a fine gold ribbon, beckons:
"Come, open this door!"

I do not refuse.
I climb past stone layers,
how they remind me of my unconscious,
take next steps into a new unknown
that would, change the rest of my life.

4

Hurd Brook Shelter

How signs, symbols, meanings of
Human Nature and Animal Nature
are connected is hard to say.

At Hurd Brook Shelter, my first stop,
Human Nature invites me
to take a short walk
from the shelter
into big pine woods
to find the "right" spot to pee.

The "spot" found me
beside the "right" tree.
I look to the ground.
My heart jumps, begins to pound!

A single, black crow feather
rests on Mother Nature's soft mossy bed.
Black as night, rainbow colors there
stream silver-grey streaks
in waning afternoon sunbeam light.

With amazement and reverence
I pick up the feather "wafer."
genuflect,
reach into its mystery,
hold this sacred gift,
between my thumb, pointer, middle finger
as I would present a communion wafer.

I raise my hand and feather
unconsciously,
high toward the sky.
My heart beats. I cry:
"This is the body of Christ
I leave you this feather at the sacred Tree,
Do this in memory of Christ for me."

The body of Christ breaks for me.
Suffering of Christ pours out for me.
More clearly, I "see."
Here, wounds heal.

Crow's communion offering is like no other.
Feather's illumined vastness
awakened by Sun's silver streaks
speaks from Crow's rainbow blackness:
"Go in Peace."

5

Crow Encounter

I.
I follow cairns up the thinning Knife Edge
when another agoraphobic panic
suddenly swirls round my head,
throws me to the ground!

I feel as if I'd be dead!
On the trail's edge
I fall between four huge chunks of granite
arranged as if my tomb!
"Is this another Abraham trick?"
"Is this my time to die, to say Goodbye?"
I look into the sky.

"Breathe," whispers Pamola's Bird Spirit.
"Eat, This is Bread of Life."
"Drink, This is the Cup of blessing."
Breath, clears my heart and head
I live! I'm not dead!

Life force remains stronger than Death force.
Death and Life are never far away.

Close they abide.
From Life and Death I receive strength
to live, breathe a lifetime of days.
Here, my existence begins!

II.
Sunshine breaks
over granite sanctuary ledge,
as if to bless my head.
Warmth gently moves my body
off Mother Earth's hard stony bed.

Morning sky above grounds me.
I curl up, quiver amid four giant granite slabs
"Great Mother" desires the best for her children.
She birthed me from Her womb.
"She fed me at Her breasts,"
sings the ancient Psalmist.

III.
"Breathe!" Relax, Eat a Cliff Bar! Drink water!"
"Life force remains stronger than death force."
My tight spinning body slows, uncoils.
I sit up.

I sense a presence above.
Soft sound of a zephyr
compels I look up
Crow floats a few feet above my head.
Crow looks straight into my eyes as if to say,
"Welcome! Glad you're not dead!"

"Perhaps an omen?"
I ask, my Self in disbelief.
"No! Give thanks, let go,"
commands my soul.
My eyes fill with tears,
Mystery is eternal.

Crow touches me
unwinds binding fears,
dreams soul out of me,
circles silently,
releases fear skyward
to Pamola's bird spirit,
leaves me a gift
of Alleluia!

Barely visible on the edge of vision,
Crow meets its partner.
I watch this couple
soar, circle, plummet,
playfully tumble through the air.
These Crows come near to say:

"Get up! Get on your feet!
You are free! Take a hike
into glorious mystery."

6

Lake Namakanta

I.
I look through the dark keyhole.
My body slows.
Trees bend, bow gently toward each other.
My sight opens cathedral doors,
beholds the apse beyond the nave.
Golden afternoon sunlight, the semicircle altar,
bring me prayerfully to my knees.
I remove my pack.

II.
I walk the center aisle
to a wide holy water-space
awesome, new, bright.
"All will be well. All will be right."

III.
Movement high in the sky
invites a view into eternity.
The dot enlarges, spirals toward me.
Bald Eagle floats down from on high!

My heart quickens as this magnificent,
message-bearing, visionary creature
eyes the place as if to say:
"Pitch your tent here tonight."

Wonder abounds!
This harbinger of grand change
beckons from some distant crossroad,
affirms my spiritual journey.
Having blessed the site,
Eagle rises silently, slowly soars out of sight.

IV.
Now come two Loons,
singing, haunting, shrill, long calls.
Their sounds echo off the moon,
fill the air with deep soulful sound.

Quietly parting water with smooth, sleek bodies,
the pair with ancient far away lineage
float to the cove to get a good look at me,
so I get a good look at them.

They sing!
Deep calls unto deep music of the spheres.
Long, beautiful echoes combine
the way organ notes combine to form one beautiful song.
Loon's sound brings God's ancient singing voice
to present time.

"Welcome to the cathedral," they say.
From ancient times to present
one great secret after another,

presents through contrasts of black and white.
"Dive in! Go deep! Take this nourishment."
Hear God's voice vibrate
through your soul from head to feet."

V.
I wade into the lake, look through the surface.
Dreams in my soul appear.
I see a bed of freshwater clams,
discover nourishment.

Seven sacred clams from mud I pluck,
fire up the Zip Stove,"
make it ready the pasta, steam these delicacies in garlic and oil.

This holy communion I did enjoy.
Sometimes I must leave worlds I know,
enter worlds of Eagle, Loon,
enjoy freshwater Clams
share a different sacred communion
in Namakanta Lake Cathedral.

7

Entering the Mystery

I rise unafraid from the tomb, reborn!
I step onto golden alchemic ribbon of trail
into great mystery of life and death.
Another "no ordinary step."

My feet want to dance.
Dance they do, a fearless dance
across that knife-like, rocky edge,
do-si-doing with trail marking, cairn icons
to "The Greatest Mountain,"
Mt. Katahdin's summit.

Changed by courage,
charged with strength renewed,
I summit Katahdin on Crow's wings.
Stand by the sign marker.
My soul opens.
North, South, East, West, Above, Below,
I'm embraced with sacred mystery by Crow.

In warm mid-morning sun
I look down the AT

as far as I can see;
give God thanks
for the unimaginable Crow gift
from the tomb pulling me.

8

The Urinal

At the lean-to
the rain stops.
I had nothing to say
to other travelers except:
"What a hell of a wet day!"

Wet tents, pitched everywhere.
Lean-to is over filled.
About my tentless situation,
a couple of guys seem to care.
They readily wiggle right and left
for me to squeeze in between.

I see the wet spot
hidden under a blanket
on damp wooden floor.
I can't ask for more.
I roll out my sleeping bag,
fall asleep listening to others snore.

Then! in the middle of the night
I feel a sprinkle
slip through its roof nail hole.

I have no place to go.
What a baptism!
Oh! what a fright!

The bearded fella next to me feels the rain.
Like dominos falling, the lean-to awakes.
Our head lamps spot this terrible plight.
My "neighbor" moves rapidly in this tight space
produces from somewhere out of sight,
a plastic urinal.

He takes string from his pack.
On a stray overhead nail, he makes a hook.
Lickety-split, strings up that urinal firm, tight
with his lightning quick thinking and Boy Scout knots;
the urinal keeps us dry the rest of the night.

Morning comes.
All hikers are surprised to see
a plastic urinal
waving in the breeze,
as if a semaphore flag alerting all others
of the nail hole in the roof that night
under the trees.

9

Waiting at "Cross" Roads

I.
The "Golden Road" cuts a destructive swath
across AT, Northeast to Southwest.
A cross forms in 100 Mile Wilderness.
Truckers, hikers pass through
these cross roads
to different purposes, different destinations.

I arrive at the cross point,
wait expectantly for brother "Laughin Thundah."
Alone, I sit contemplating this internal juncture.
Dross of my life bubbles.
My old oak rolltop desk displays
a stout, two-inch-thick, wood cross.
The exposed silver Corpus,
hangs naked.
No single facial feature
betrays his human figure.

Jesus' head lifts skyward.
Over his right shoulder
far beyond Eagle's vision.

He speaks in silence:
"I am here for all humanity.
My body will be dead. I will not die."

II.
I see myself in Jesus' face
as I see my Self in faces I see.

Fate leads to many a crossroad.
Here, fate reminds me
I hike to face cosmic mystery.

Jesus takes on Shadow
of "what might have been,"
offers radical new hope,
transforms suffering beyond agony.
Healing hope is within my scope.

I am "treasure in this earthen vessel,"
eyes open, heart expectant.
Here now on the AT
I am called, Crow Feathah!

In Creation's great forest cathedral,
"orchestra extraordinaire"
sends music of the spheres
though verdant fresh air.

Beethoven's 9th symphony
surrounds, plays
"Joyful, Joyful, We Adore Thee."

Thrills my open heart with radical hope:
something new from empty tombs,
something new arises off the cross.
Silent "seeing" clears.

Playful Crows, Eagle vision,
soulful Loons, shy Deer
form a sacred choir,
set free hope divine,
open heart, mind.

Treasure expands sacred atmosphere.
Priceless elements are here.
I wait for Thundah,
reflect, pray, give thanks for wonder
of being alive, just being here!

Death ruminates, dissipates.
Death is not "dead." Death is "Alive Mortality."
I step south from "cross roads"
into the New Creation I AM!

To this crossroad comes Laughing Thundah,
companion, witness, hiker, friend,
Hope Bearer, who brings
his journey tucked in his pack
to hike with my journey.
I wonder, How will it end?

10

Unlikely Beginning

We stand at the hotel tie rack, laugh, joke,
decide which gaudy discounted necktie to buy.
After chatter and prattle about awful colored ties,
Denis asks out of the clear blue sky:
"Want to hike the Appalachian Trail with me?"

Stunned!
After a thoughtful pause, I reply:
"Yes! Yes, indeed!
Before I die, I want to hike the AT."

We affirm our agreement, with purchase
of similar silly ties
decorated with slanty colored bars
of purple, blue and red
to celebrate our brotherhood
to hike the AT
before we're dead!

We take a few short hikes to check each other out,
determine if we are compatible inside and outside
to make this journey, yet still have our skin.

We summit Katahdin,
test our knees, scrape up our bodies,
take a healing "time out."

In unspoken ways of midlife men,
our inside wants outside, our outside wants in.
I don't know what the path will bring,
where cairns will guide.
At this Cross Road
We're ready for "time-in."

A witness watches, observes,
has ears to hear, eyes to see,
"Hope seeds" to spread,
nurture to birth.
Laughin Thundah, my witness, will be!

I leave work a day life behind,
To walk separately, together, alone.
Into myself I continue this
2,190-mile 10-year section hike,
epic tale of transformation
down the Appalachian Trail.

11

Barcelona Dream Poem--Blue Blaze

The way it is, is not the way it was
in my dream last night
as I slept in Barcelona.

I walk the Appalachian Trail
on a bumpy, lumpy path
through wispy fields of tall bent grass
in Western Maine low lands
on a hot, humid summer day.

At a crossing, I see broken bones
of table, benches, chair
scattered around fire-pit stones.
Someone left this unholy mess:
"Dank" smells like a smelly old sheet
hang in the air
at the simple intersection here.

To this miserable, unwelcome sight.
from my pack I take
a roll of old recycled shoe string
to sew up broken wounds.

With square knots, clove and half hitches,
I repair, mend broken pieces
with dozens and dozens of shoe string stitches.
Knot after knot I wind old laces,
Bind, splint wooden rounds, detached seats, and legs,
to put "Humpty Dumpty" together again.

Now, the cat and fiddle can make new music
as they jump over the moon
and watch with amazement the little dog laugh
so dishes of hikers
can't run away with spoons.

Instead, these weary walkers
sit, rest, take off their socks,
dry them on fire-hot rocks;
fill their bowls, nourish their souls,
so when Deep Calls Unto Deep
Hikers will know:
it's time to get up on their feet.
It's time to get back on the trail.
No more broken seats.
No more broken bones.

No more "diddle, diddling,
the cat's done fiddling.
The Little Dog's done laughing at this magical scene.

The cow's still wondering why it wasn't jumping
as the Dish in my backpack rests easily with the Spoon.
I turn to the trail with renewed vigor and vim.
The way it was, is not the way it is.

12

Wind, Rain, and Death

I emerge from dreamtime.
Wind blows, hits the cliff with mighty force.
Immovable strength of Earth's foundation
turns, powers that force
up a sheer rock face into our faces.
We move dangerously
at a very slow pace.

This wind is no Zephyr,
no soothing breeze.
This wind is angry,
wants to bring us to our knees.

Heads bent toward the ground.
Close to cliff's edge, we shoulder through
unexpected, wind-driven, pelting rain
weather stew.

With mighty lungs,
wind puffs out cheeks as far as they can puff.

Pursing lips as far as they can purse,
almost blow our bodies off the earth.
We move slowly along this precarious course.

Wind takes advantage,
another breath, sucks in air,
fills its cheeks full again.
Wind lets go, blows hard and harder,
rips open our ponchos,
nearly pulls those rain covers right off our packs.
On feet of fear we stumble about,
dreading a fall,
or a tumble over the high cliff wall.
Words slam to mind:
"All journeys have secret destinations
of which the traveler is unaware."

I am here now, blown around,
wherever wind desires.
I dance again with death's mystery.
Is death "now" my secret destination?

Am I to discover the secret
before this great trail adventure begins?
Or are these wind-blown steps
overture to some powerful new adventure?

I do not want to take a life ending-tumble.
The storm, the wind, the rain make me humble.
Mother Nature shows her power and surprise.
Adventure opens my eyes.

Wind screams: "Beware!
Be aware of wildness, its dangers.
Be adventurous, dare.
Take care.
Don't let great expectations
confound limitations, spoil your journey.
Respect limitations.
Let strength and power bring good care,
enrich your spirit of adventure, "Beware!"

13

Entry into Mahoosucs

I. Encounter
I enter the Creator's Mahoosucs
to hike a beautiful range of midsize blue mountains
where streams, ponds, pleasant valleys
create a painting worthy to be hung
in any museum gallery.

These 28 miles cross the boundary
between Maine and New Hampshire,
follow south white blazes
over and under giant boulders and rocks
to AT's toughest mile and a half,
Mahoosuc Notch.

I lean into Notch mystery,
wonder what Adam felt
when in paradise, on a high peak he knelt,
saw awe-inspiring lands,
combinations of space and color,
blue and white, light and dark.
as he began
his journey into God's land.

II. Shadow-Moon meeting

I'm grateful,
for what happened behind me:
wounded knee, stone tomb, loon,
Crow, Eagle, windy cliff,
wind-blown brush with death.

Darkness pulls me
to face beginnings of a different kind.
No place to hide
from inner life revelations beyond my ken.
Shadow invites
seeing what I do not want to see:
the black hole where I hide to ignore how
dark confrontations galore point to light.
I have nothing to lose. Everything to gain.
Today, something feels different inside.
Mother Nature's voice, though silent,
speaks healing sounds from Shadow catacombs,
deep under ground.
Different energy awakens!
A new section begins.

III. Moon

"There's the full Moon!"
The Old Fella gently casts light and shadow
over Mahoosuc peaks,
down slopes along the Trail.
"Old Man" is very wise.
He sees my Shadow,
the disguise I carry in my eyes

to hide fears,
tears I feel in inside.

The "Old Fellah" rises higher and higher,
glows brighter and brighter, illumines my front side,
warms my eyes, hugs my heart with mystery, wonder.
Behind me stands Shadow, black
hiding the path and my overfilled pack.

IV. Keyhole

Morning's Shadow Light pulls me off the bluff
through a dark Earthen keyhole
where visible and invisible
struggle, to strip away disguises,
darken inner light,
hinder freedom.
The "Old Man" slips behind Western hills.
Slowly I go, deeper beyond the keyhole.
Light fades to blackness.
I wonder, "Does the key give me confidence
to make passage into my soul?"
I don't know.

V. Key

Truth is, I have the key.
It's all up to me.
If those disguises fall away, what would I see?
Who would I be? Would I be the real me?
By asking right questions, I'll see."

On the edge of invisibility
I discover a tiny snowfield
with just enough visibility

to see Laughin Thundah,
and just enough room to stand.

Smack! Surprise! Right Questions!
An unexpected ice-ball cracks me in the chest!
Ancient snow Crystals splatter across my vest!
True to his name, Trickster, Thundah,
stands laughing in the dark!
We throw at each other ancient, frozen snowballs,
with playful hearts.

Our fun is done. Challenge begins.
To our knees we twist, bow, bend.
Now, on our bellies,
between boulders pulling our packs
we squeeze through a black,
tight little keyhole on our backs.
No shades of gray here, not even a white blaze.

Damp, wet, cold,
the hard icy granite path is black.
Nearly puts me in a daze.
I scuff my knuckles, hands and face.
I wriggle on my side
use every muscle, strain every sinew
to drag myself through this
invisible claustrophobic place.
Energy drains. My body stiffens.
I move slower and slower.
Breath labors. Mind tingles. Fear increases.
Will I die? Will I live?
Just when I feel I might die
on this path of fears and tears,

somewhere in this dark invisible place
a trickle sound, I hear:

"Though I walk through the valley
of the Shadow of death
I will fear no evil.
Your rod and your staff comfort me."

Confused, my whole body, mind, spirit quicken.
In black ahead,
I see a pinhole of light
penetrate the dark.

"You prepare a table before me
In the presence of my enemies.
You anoint my head with oil,
My cup brims over."

Light grows brighter.
Drips get louder.
It's a stream!
A tiny ice melt stream and light beam!
"Click", the keyhole unlocks.

Reassurance glows
with goodness and mercy.
This dawning realization feels crazed.
On tunnel's rock face
I see a hopeful white blaze!

Ah! How goodness and kindness pursue me
Every day of my life;

My home, the house of the lord,
Endures forever!

A white blaze Key is hidden in my pack!
When historic fears are invisible to me,
I am invisible to myself.
I must invite fear out.

On the "killer mile and one half"
mostly on belly & back,
white blazes guide through Shadow black.
Something softens within.
Odd energy emerges.
What is hidden becomes visible.
I carry the Key: I must Trust me.
This Shadow-Moon encounter
opens the door.
My pack,
loaded with historic fears,
brings light.
No longer invisible,
I walk with visible smile,
exit the Notch keyhole
with new meaning for life.

14

Weight of Generations

I.
On Agiocochook summit
in mid-August,
there is no snow . . .
only White Mountain majesty,
accepting God's universality.

Here on the summit,
lines of multicolored people, races,
speaking different languages
come to see "Big A's" grand importance.
Carriages, cars, vans, buses fill parking lots,
for the circus here on the "Big Top."

Loafers, high heels,
rush here and there to find the restroom.
Tourists push, hurry,
squawk like barnyard chickens,
to get their selfies standing at the summit;
drive home, tell their friends they've done it.

These "mountain climbers" want to be seen,
with a centerpiece photo,
the old black Cog Railway engine,
as it hisses and whistles pulling into the "tent."

This "Big Top" circus scene,
bewilders, pains.
God wants people and earth to be one.
Deep down people want the same.

Visitors disrespect summit's glory
and one another. They don't whisper,
let their souls be touched by "Big Top Wonder,"
instead look past awe and majesty,
to the next stop on travel agendas.

In this grand, wonderful high place,
I hang my head,
weep with the Mountain,
witness earth's suffering, pain.

II.
I walk off the summit, find a quiet, vacant spot,
sit down on a "hard to find" sunny rock.
The view southwest,
slows my breath, expands my chest,
quiets inner space to rest, reflect.

Out of deep black—
blacker than cog's black steaming engine—
"Giant One" no longer can bear
the weight of generations. . .
Balance gives way! I slide off my quiet spot

hit another rock,
fall hard on my ass.

Pain feels like soul-breaking window glass
shattering across my back.

Abuse
I'm a preadolescent boy,
a mixed up, tragic PTSD mess.
Unconscious shame, guilt, evil, sin
are unbearable in my nascent mind.
Wrongs I experience are ferocious!
Boyhood, innocent identity is stolen.
I'm alone, broken, hungry for protection.

Trauma hidden memories
erupt like a volcano
flow tears down my face
the way Ammonoosuc stream flows
from summit to base.

Neighbor Abuse
Wilford's Chris-Craft gleams.
Its reddish mahogany allures,
says, "Come to me. I'll take you for a ride."
A different engine's full-throated rumble draws me closer.
"Hop in," Wilford cajoles.
"I'll take you for a ride, my boy."
I hop in.

Effortless, the classy boat
knifes through helpless water
leaving behind big foamy wake.

Air waters, blurs my eyes.
I like the wind on my face.

"Sit on my lap so you can see better."
I'm a big deal with hands on the wheel.

Tricked, by false affection,
Seduced by unbridled, unprotected attention,
I'm confused by hunger for affection,
experience of pleasure.

Priest Abuse
Priest befriends me,
a young student.
He seduces me to a
fine dinner at Boston Park Plaza
to discuss
a summer student chaplaincy
in Yosemite.
Unaccustomed to such largesse,
I overate, over-drank,
found myself with priest hands
on my body ready to rape.
I cried out "NO!"
I stumbled to hotel lobby,
gave my phone number to the night clerk.
He saw my condition. Made the call.
A roommate drove me home.
I felt like I'd lost, my face, my soul.

Teaching Preacher Abuse
I am husband for two years, father of one,
new pastor with empty pockets,

learning preaching techniques.
On his nickel,
teaching preacher invited me to a preaching conference,
to learn preaching-trade tricks.
Said we could share a two-bed room.
I went to bed.
He returned from the bathroom,
came to my bed-side.
In a soft seductive voice, he said:
"I want to join you in bed."
I had no place to hide.
"NO!" I shouted, "I don't want you in my bed!
Get out! Get away!"

By three pedophilic men
I am raped, sexually abused, traumatized.
Why does sexual abuse keep happening to me?

I don't understand.
I'm bewildered, confused.
Such behavior is wrong!
At Norwich at Andover Newton I hide,
search dark library corners,
research human sexuality books
to find answers to this profound question.

Now I walk the AT
carry unconscious weight of generations.
On Agiocochook windows, doors explode!
Shame shatters.
Horizon emerges behind a foggy veil.
I seek this hike for God's inner peace.

15

Frozen

I.
Anxiety locks me up.
I freeze for years not feeling.
Family echoes resonate:
"You never do anything right."
"You are never good enough."

Back then, felt worth was measured:
"I am a sexual object of 'love fraud.'"
Shame torches unworthiness.
Flames flare in a forest of guilt.
Shame explodes with earthquake force,
burns open, ruins my young soul.
I live under a forest canopy
filled with cigar smoke, not a father's love.
This wound I carry in my pack today.

II.
I confront evil:
Stand up! Speak the secret!
Demand: "Take me Home!"
Let "the Sacred," however humans name it,

Buddha, Shiva, God, Bhagavan,
guide my steps to healing goodness.
Let petunia's healing fragrance
guide through fog.
Fear not "Shadow of Death,"
Walk through darkness
knowing waters of Your Creation's musical spheres
shed white light beams along the trail,
pass on hope to next generations.
May strong Oaks pass on strength,
golden Maple colors sweeten dark times,
open hope, comfort mystery.
To myself I must be true.

16

Ridges--Crawford Path

Some say Agiococook's summit is
Cloud home to White Cloud Hermit
whose open gate welcomes
hikers, travelers, seekers alike
through dark night,
white sun daylight.

I drop from the summit
to Appalachian Trail contiguous with Crawford path
along a beatific, wide-open mountain ridge
into Crawford Notch.
Trail and Path are one
till Crawford Path stops,
AT passes through.

A change in gait provides
body respite for mind to loosen
from "good/bad," "right/wrong" thinking.
This release calms my heart rate gate,
opens trust, wonder, freedom,
a living unity.

Opposites push unity away.
I'm afraid I push others away.
Connections get lost in this mercurial raid.
Hope received on Katahdin weakens.
Crow's presence is distant.
Thundah's friendship thins.
"Slow walking" a ridge path,
summit and valley invite reopening
gates within.

Amazed, how such ideas come about;
how head and heart turn inside out,
open life.

My view expands into horizon,
to tangle with life's big questions.
Slow walking invites reflection.

What's hiding inside my Self
under layers of veneer?
What do I seek?
What's my destiny?
Who am I?

An answer comes through White Cloud Hermit's
ancient words of the prophet:

"Those who hope in the Lord will renew their strength.
They will soar on wings like eagles.
They will run and not be weary.
They will walk and not faint."

I'm tired out! torn apart!
Knocked down! Freedom stifled!
Inner judge strikes down a gavel hard,
causes relationships not to travel.

Everything belongs!
In all Creation everything belongs!
Everything is relationship!
Everything is connection!
Wounds can heal!
Hope shines as confirmation!

What is my path from mid-life to everlasting?
When I go high to a summit, God is there.
In valleys of depth, God is there.
When I ridge-walk, I transform,
inner gates swing wide open.
Opposites integrate.
Shared words strive to be spoken.

This inspiration offers a different vision.
I see horizon.
God is here and there.
No need hiding behind iron grates.
Inward, alone, I die.
Loving I live.
Love walks through both gates.

17

Lake of the Clouds

Moon's beams embrace Lake of the Clouds.
Lake's surface opens, receives
Moon's Light.

Moon and Lake embrace.

I embrace Lake and Moon.
What a beautiful sight!
What a wondrous Love!

18

John Garvin: Celebration of Life

Magic, mystery, challenge,
fun hiking with companions
I journey south from Mt. Katahdin,
along Appalachian Trail.

John Garvan convinces Thundah and me
his physical shape and condition
is strong enough to hike a four-day section
from Lonesome Lake Hut
to Rt. 25 Glencliff intersection.

John comes late to the hut.
In muddy, soggy ruts did he get stuck?
Did he slip on slippery rocks?
A slip like that would surely stop his "clock."

I wait no longer. It's time for tea.
I'm about to tack up a note to a tree.
Then, in the distance, I see coming up a rise,
a giant slow-moving pack.

Closer the pack moves up the path,
sight of John emerges,
his load bending him into the hill.

It's hard to know
who carries that pack on his back
it hides him so.
Bulged inside and out, it's stacked tall!
Every step he takes
pushes more sweat from his brow.
We meet. We greet. John drops his burden
so his senses he will not lose.

John must be reliving his old sailor days
when he went to sea with a big sailor pack:
Two quarts of water. A quart of milk.
Enough clothes for a week.
Two cans of tuna. A tarp, a tent
I told him not to bring.

A packaged hank of clothesline, a bottle of wine,
to "make our voices sing, imaginary bells ring."
Overweighted with food. Overladen with gear,
John sincerely remarks:
"I just want to lighten your load
and bring you hearty good cheer."

"Are your feet sore?" I ask.
"They're okay," he said the way a guy would.
"Let's take a look." I look. "Certainly not okay!"
"More food. They look like hamburger," I say!

We perform first aid, return feet to his boots.

I lighten his load. Put his extras in my pack.
I take the clothesline; the heavy bottle of wine.
We limp to Kinsman Pond. He throws off his pack,
goes into the lean-to. Slides into his bag, lies on his back.

Boys in the shelter take one look.
They don't even laugh.
We break out tuna, open the wine.
For all in the lean-to, we fine dine.
Thundah cooks more garlic.
Someone dices carrots. Another peels potatoes.
Fortunately, John did not bring tomatoes.
Water boils, is nice and hot.
Now everything goes in one pot.
For all there's plenty.
The boys eat their fill. Clean up the mess.
Time to rest.
To their audience the boys did tell all sorts of stories.
We thank them profusely for post-culinary good cheer
by off-loading as much food, frivolous gear as we can
to these strong cheerful young fellows
on verge of becoming men.

Morning comes with rising sun over Mt. Lafayette.
John bandaged his feet,
gave more extras to the boys,
decided four days would become one.

So, John with his very light pack
Headed back down to Franconia Notch
where his unfortunate hike
would come to a stop.

PART II: DISCOVERY

19

Beethoven and Kancamagus

I
I drive the old car
across the "Kank" at dawn in June of '95.
Fog lifts from valleys, creates a pictorial symphony
of organ pipes among mountain tops
as "feathers", "horse tails"
float music in sunny blue sky.
I feel alive!

Content, beauty is all around me.
I feel gratitude for all I see.
The dawning morning empty road
directs my way to N. Conway
to meet Thundah,
begin our next section
on the AT.

II
"Click."
I slide the CD into the dash.

In a flash Beethoven's Ninth flows,
crowns white mountain ash
as soft, gentle notes
begin their stair climb
to glorious crescendos, music divine!

Creation's voices sing!
Bells and timbrels ring!
Horns and trumpets proclaim
God's wondrous musical gift of creation
to all humanity!

My heart explodes!
I'm in joyous beyond!
Space and time attune,
Harmonize, become one!

I stop the car. Step out of my body!
I soar heavenward in eternal air
through Beethoven's soul.
Tears stream down my face.
I meet God face to face.
I live, alive! I Hike Alive!

I don't know how
I arrive in this jubilant moment.
I do know, I want to live and die
immersed in such mysterious, joyous space:
Please, when I die, please:
Let Beethoven's melody ring,
Let H. van Dyke's words sing:

Joyful, Joyful, we adore thee
God of glory, God of love.
Hearts unfold like flowers before thee
opening to the sun above.

It's a great day to die!

(Melody: Ludwig van Beethoven; Words: Henry van Dyke)

20

White Cliff Rocks--Father's Day

I.
Two midlife hikers trudge down the AT,
follow every white blaze through dreary haze.
Thundah's storm is up and away.
Sun is out! We give a hearty shout!

At White Rock Cliffs, we take a sit.
"Some people sit and think," said the old Vermonter,
"Others just sit."
"I'll sit. You think," I said to Thundah.
Both of us give way to wonder.

II.
We each have two sons.
Our fathers died young when we were young.
Today we take time out to honor our dads,
time we never had.

Three generations of boys and fathers.
Memories and legacies from past times we gather.

Feelings to sort.
So much to remember, grieve, that can be fixed.

Ancient wisdom says: "Sons live out
unlived lives of their fathers,
who lived out unlived lives of fathers before them."
Thundah's dad died at 55. My dad died at 56.

Their lives were cut short,
lacked enough time to fully thrive.
Unfinished business left unsaid,
hidden behind zipper flaps.
Here, we unzip, open, free up
lighten our packs.

III.
A distant motor sound distracts.
An antique biplane flies into my head.
Childhood biplane memories
soar through my mind.
Dad takes me to Augusta air show.
Dad and I stand together watch double-wingers.
Hands touch, emotions soar
through air down here, up there!

Thundah speaks. He too watched double wingers
zoom and soar
do their stuff; power straight up to a dead stop.
Drop straight down, do a loop-de-loop,
just missing the ground,
landing exactly in the right spot!
Such memories with our dads
are gold nuggets,

special, deeply precious
we remember, share with each other.

The Montreal Special whistles
from valley's bottom.
Wheels rumble along the tracks, clickity clack.

Filled with hungry memories,
it's funny how memories sit within
like an acorn waiting to be born.
A sound or smell pops off acorn's top.
Pressure releases with the sound of a horn
sometimes a whistle.

IV.
At 15, Thundah hops a freight in Pittsfield, MA.
A message from inside comes into his head:
"Leave home, be a hobo, be free,
ride the rails, let a freight car be your bed."

Thundah hides under a freight car
in the Albany rail yard.
He is seen!
A voice from a yard worker calls out:
"Go home and grow up!
You don't want to sleep in the rain,
especially under a train."

"That rail yard worker
gave me the best advice
I ever received." said Thundah.
"Here am I!"

V.
I drift in my memory
to a line of colorful painted circus cars
that chug, chug along tracks
by the Kennebec River.
Elephant's trunk wraps around
the circus car's iron bars.
Giraffe's head pokes through
its special giraffe car roof.
The head looks like a periscope
to us kids sitting on the front stoop.

I run wild with my two brothers and sister,
all around the front yard
like the tiger wishes he could.
We shout, scream,
wave arms and hands to animal attendants.
View from the river bank
provides front row seats.
Spectacular! Just Grand!

At times Dad joins in.
Plays with us. Is one of us.
Without fallout, my sibs and I
delight to see him, a little wild child.
The circus train moves on
up tracks to Augusta fairground.

White Rock Cliffs is a conscious diving board
into unconscious life for Thundah and me.
Here, in the sea of loss,
grief, demons, dragons
release Father's Day memories

with other shining miracles of wonder.
Thundah and I heft our packs to our backs.
Communion between two men ends.
We chug chug along our AT journey.

21

Aria and Hope--Blue Blaze

I
All over the world novel coronavirus attacks,
knocks out humans through personal contact.
Covid takes away breath,
leaves families faced with a loved one's tragic death.

II
In the middle of Maine woods
lives a young girl named Aria.
"She is a Princess" with spirit of "lumin-Aria."
She confronts coronavirus with heart music and grace.
Aria gathers family this sun-filled Sunday afternoon
to enlighten them and the whole human race.

We meet through magical world of Zoom
on five different Zoom screens for afternoon delight.
We will enjoy as one, musical family fun.
Coronavirus heaviness we will put on the run.

The Zoom clan gathers at their screens.
Grandparents, Aunt, cousins arrive.

Greetings, happy faces,
words of anticipation create chatter of sound
as this concert audience finds its place.
Mom, Dad, Brother place their chairs.
Alive with expectation, family gets front row seats,
in majestic yurt's magic, warm, comfortable space.
For them to see the show live is a special treat.

The rest of us wait before our screens
for the imaginary curtain call,
when the beautiful young artist,
enters this lovely music hall.
Curtain rises.
Audience breathes deeply, settles into chairs.
Smiles on little square Zoom screens
reveal a family who cares.
Aria takes her bow, turns, faces the piano.
Delicate hands and fingers lift.
Clunky sound of computer keys transform
Aria's musical gift into glorious sounds of piano keys.

First notes of Pachelbel's Canon rise,
drift beyond yurt's door,
to sow musical hope seeds
in a sad, fearful world.
From "Yurtdom" to Spain to Richmond, New Hampshire,
for people all over the world,
Aria's notes join, come alive,
hope flows into our lives.

Aria embraces this virus with music!
For those captured, quarantined,
for those listening,

musical joy turns our hearts soft, tender
hearing this young pianist's gift
as we listen with heart and soul.

There are times when little things mean more,
than music of a big grand marching band.
With heart and soul, Aria shares her enriching gifts,
with family, with others all over the world.

Thank you, Aria, for your gift!
I love you.

Grampa
April 12, 2020

22

Zig Zag Troya
Dream--Blue Blaze

I.
It's middle of 2020 Great Pandemic.
I live quarantined in Denia.
I sneak out to "Troya."
the neighborhood mom-and-pop-store,
to get a loaf of bread, a bottle of wine.

Two miles, I walk zig-zag, hide on back streets
so "cops" don't catch me on my feet,
tell me: "Go straight home. Get off the street!"

I look over my shoulder,
arrive at the "T" intersection:
50 yards to Troya.
At the "T" I stop. Freeze!
I can't walk fifty steps farther.

This "stop" is the story of my life!
Near end of battle with blame and shame,
I procrastinate it victory, its finish.

Not everything I diminish.
Many things I diminish.

I lacked adolescent courage
to tell this horrible story.
Shame crystallized life-blood,
frozen for years by blame.
Harsh anguish of inner pain I did not feel.
The harder my body trained to "win,"
the deeper my real being hid,
wounded, in the belly
of the Greek wooden horse
beneath wooden skin.

Even ancient gods and God didn't respond.
My inner life plodded along
inside the Aegean creature,
till one day I told myself:
"I am a prepubescent victim of sexual abuse.
No more self-abuse!"

II.
That night, I cross the "T," turn right.
Onward to "Troya!"
In dark, laden with pain,
I cut open horses' belly,
drop down the wood door,
move down ramps of shame,
ready to battle blame.

No longer will I let abuse impact
life, marriages, relationships!

With courage I'll tell my story.

One after the other
I called four regarded psychotherapists.
Each doctor ignored
my emotionally wounded self.
Each abruptly said "No,"
left me at the ramp
with no therapy agreement
to battle sexual abuse.

I press on, keep going toward "Troya,"
"Zig" hike high, "zag" deep.
Change happens.
Doors open.
New directions,
lead me out of the horse
into analysis with an analyst.
I discover different angles
to disentangle messy wounds of
sexual abuse, shame, blame.

Now, I write this Epic,
sit at table where bread and wine
transform night's black evil into
Shadowy tapestry of star shapes,
telling ancient stories of healing, of hope.
I press on beyond these 50 yards,
repair, heal my soul's longing for itself.
Ultreia!

23

God's Gentle Knock

I.
Trails are ancient. Trails are archetypal.
Trails take me through our planet's clock cycles.
Trails swim me to bottom of the sea.
From my mother's womb water,
I take my first journey.
Seventy-eight years later,
I "press on" from Troya.
I live! Here I AM!
Awake from unconscious sleep,
on White Rocks Cliffs,
I accept,
the blaze of "Grace!"

The Blue Blaze of "Planes and Trains,"
that fated Father's Day,
become an inner place
where doors to sorrow open gates.

Those blazes in past years
I did not recognize.
I walked by.

I could not discover what I did not know long ago.
My soul can't go where it doesn't want to go.
I write now at AT - Long Trail junction,
where this epic tale unites,
becomes one trail of hope, even delight.

II.
From this junction I walk two trails,
as they zig-zag back and forth together,
to release inner brokenness
weave one hope trail,
as it straddles the life-death-life boundary!

Sometimes, I'm more on "Life" side.
Sometimes, I'm more on "Death" side.
Sometimes, I move slow or fast.
Other times, in seminary class,
I become unmasked.

I still see a blaze in those seminary halls
illuminate inner trails of
meaning soul, spirit
through troubling haze.

Ancient trails,
marked by rocks, slashes on trees meander.
Sometimes cairns show the way.
Modern trails like the AT are painted with ease.
Two-by-six-inch slaps of white, blue, yellow,
even red paint make
those blazes easier to see.

24

I Take the Dive--Long Trial

God didn't lose me.
Early on, I lost my way.
God invites, keeps inviting.

On White Rocks Cliffs
I stand at diving board's end,
conscious, ready to dive in
swim alive in deep valleys of collective unconscious.

Rise high to mountain-tops of creation's mystery.
The time has come to blend
AT- LT to one
contiguous healing wonder.
God's knocks gently.
I walk down the "center aisle."

25

Pillow Talk

I wake from dream time.
Starburst colors flood my eyes.
I lie still in bed.
"You can do this," a voice from the pillow said.
"Let go of *Yellow Rose of Texas*.
Confront the wound you did not invite."

Meaning from Troya I hear in my heart:
"Press on regardless! Press on with your heart!"
Knock down the door.
Let fly the criminal theater scene.
Enter heart energy!
Heal hidden wounds once and for all!
Dispense sexual abuse strife.
Empty that old pack!
Hike Alive! Transform to new life!"

26

Mt. Greylock Autumn

I.
To hike or not to hike,
The day is grey.
Indifference tires, drains fire
from mind, body, spirit systems.

First mile "up" perhaps I'll wake up.
Trail is wet. Rocks slippery.
Between earth and person, little connection.
Inner wounds nag me down,
like a down-fall of logs
strewn over the ground.

Inwardly, I see myself curl up
under a log like a fetus.
Perhaps a burst of energy will hit me,
blast away dirt.
Maybe I'll see Jesus.

II.
I walk into the 3,489-foot-high parking lot.
No Jesus!

A 93-foot crumbling phallic
Massachusetts Veterans
War Memorial tower
instead stands erect.

Tower grey, locked up.
A repressed memory flashes.
Awful sexual abuse trauma
again explodes before my eyes.
A sign hangs from chains, reads:
"reconstruction, repairs, restoration."
"That's me!" Contiguous trails
describe healing work of individuation.

Inscribed words on a memorial plaque read:

"They were faithful even to death.
A new eternal light shines enough
to shine to the stars and back,
shines with hope, memorializes
those wounded, and died."

Crumbled childhood is lost.
Eternal light is dim. I feel dead.
In grief I hang my head,
for veterans and for me.

27

Departing Mt. Greylock

Sun melts night the way it melts
ice and snow in morning light.
Over ice, I slip down the trail.
Frosty edges cover Berkshire hills glorious tapestry
with a silvery fringed glow.

Solace fills my heart with natural comfort,
of earth's multi-color sight!
I walk amazed with wonder
God's Natural Cathedral brings.

God is everywhere!
God is the cold, the ice, the snow!
God is pain of hell, breath of life.
Across the valley, God's Creation is aglow!

I lift my arms, my face to celebrate
this outdoor worship space.
Appalachian Trail memories of hope
unlock "something" within.

Healing waters stir.
Repair, reconstruction, restoration begin.

Ice melts, cracks, echoes,
Kank's highway symphony of hope.
Crow and Eagle's playfulness;
Laughing Thundah's witness,
embrace God's grace with us;
Mahoosuc moon guides
into starlit inner space.
I'm coming out of the weeds!
I'm beginning to feel!
Repair, reconstruction, restoration, heal.
New growth churns within,
I hear Mahoosuc spring water
bubble, sing of Baptism.
Ground of my being awakens.

All Life is Sacred
Title of my first sermon, 10/15/1969

28

Communion at John's House

My feet make tracks to John's house
where Thundah, Stick, and I,
refresh strength and power
with a nice hot shower.

John's, daughter Emily,
my wife, Pilar, provide a hot meal
with special congratulatory flair.

Something beyond my knowing
is about to happen.
Table is set with bread, wine, spaghetti
Joyful friends laugh heartily.
We are ready to celebrate, not just reunion.
We are ready to celebrate a special communion.

Mountain tops, rivers, fall colors brilliance
transform consciousness, heal.
God's revelations come through Creation.

Sacredness consecrates this table.
As God is present with Jesus and his friends,
God is present between friends here.
This ordinary table of thanksgiving
is a table of healing mystery.
"Eat, drink and be thankful:"
Words to remember throughout history.

29

Pandemia in Denia--Blue Blaze

I'm locked up in Spain
at the beginning and end of another tale.

Pilar is my mate on *this* journey.
We are trapped in Denia
by 2020 coronavirus "pandemia."

We must be careful. We must be wise.
We are not yet ready to die.
We wear our masks, cover our faces, glove our hands.
Walk 3 feet apart, protect ourselves as best we can.

Plane tickets home are cancelled three times.
We have no idea when we'll be out of this bind.
We are locked in! Tied by a Gordian Covid knot!
We don't want to be caught!

Ninety days granted by my visa
have already gone by.
I'm here ninety days more

because planes to the USA can't fly.
No vapor trails do I see in clear blue sky.

Nobody knows how long Covid-19 will last.
I see masks and more masks, blue rubber gloves
everywhere. By this virus no one wants to die.
Everyone searches for healing White Doves.
This 2020 novel coronavirus makes me cry.

30

Telling Truth--Blue Blaze

I'm trapped wondering "If I *will:*
Die in Denia."
Death by this horrible pandemic killer
buries daily thousands of bodies in the ground.
Death's numbers by this thriller are profound.

Grievers grieve by the thousands.
Health worker's brows furrow.
For patients, for the world, caregivers sacrifice
with hearts of generous compassion.

Creation is weighted down.
Cataclysm, catharsis, change happen.
Numbers of Deaths and contagious
tell of external physical casualties are outrageous.
Photos, films of agonized faces
show interior emotional tragedy.
Every nation and our one world
stand paralyzed by hungry corona contagion.

I stand in high places peering into dream time.
Look down, see humans milling around

in a state of helpless delusion,
weighted heavy with loss, grief, confusion.
Helpless, not knowing what to do,
people linger in illusions.

This dream scene strikes loud, painful clangs within
as I stand on our Spanish window balcony
banging pots and pans supporting health care workers.
I look into a mirror take a deep breath, a memory emerges.
In vision "beyond" I see "outer" world of Trail.
"Below" I see loss, grief, mourning.

Sixty-eight years ago, a much older man
seduces, sexually abuses me.
Traumatized,
my life was set
on a very different *Blue Blaze* trail destiny.

The dream mirror reflects "out there"
the world of all creation.
The plaza below shows
"inner worlds" of heart, humanity.
In "heart" I see horrible dark isolation
with traumatic lifelong wounding.

Here, again,
I walk two blazed trails at once
amidst coronavirus pandemic.
My overloaded pack holds Covid 19 contagion
along with childhood sexual abuse.
My inner pack weighs heavy with
confusion, blame, shame, guilt.

31

Ultimate Affection

May Mediterranean air receives
crematory stack smoke,
spreads material particles to infinite everywhere.
Please cremate me if coronavirus kills me.
Let stack smoke curl into air,
my material particles
float into "Infinite Everywhere."

NO!
Wait!
I'm already there!
God IS everywhere!
I let this great Appalachian Trail lesson drift off,
if only for a moment, like smoke in air.

NO!
Where I'm embraced,
smoke particles of my cremating body
curl in every direction
into Ultimate Affection.

32

Family History--Blue Blaze

I.
Wehrwein means "protector of the vineyard."
Wehrwein family "Vineyard."
does not protect "grapes" well.
"What's wrong with you!"
echoes the family refrain.
"What's wrong with you!"

Unprotected, violated, sinned against,
I suffer horrible sexual abuse tragedy
alone by the lake in "Paradise,"
under that snake entwined "Tree."

Too young to "see"
what "knowledge" means.
Guilt, shame steal my heart.
I need understanding, protection, support,
not debilitating grief of a broken heart.

II.
God didn't will Wilford
to pull wool over my parent's eyes,
God didn't will my parents not to protect me.
The predator claimed me for himself
used false love to trash my life.

My parents, trapped in "mud" of their unworthiness,
did not read inner signs
passed to them by their parents,
who in turn, passed on to me,
a lack of protection, love, care,
amidst crippling uncertainty.

33

Take Me Home--Blue Blaze

I.
Time comes. I tell perpertraitor Devil:
"TAKE ME HOME! TAKE ME HOME!"
No more Chris-Craft rides:
My inner child finds strength
to cast out demon-bastard Wilford!

I walk out of night's darkness up home's lit walk
lined with blooming petunias standing at attention:
"Welcome home!"
Sweet petunia fragrance
embraces, offers hope.
Mom hugs.
Dad smiles, lays his hand on my shoulder.
Insides explode. Tears flow...
Abuse is over!

II.
Months later, Dad sits at breakfast
with coffee and morning paper:

"Gary, please come here."
He points to the daily KJ court news:

"Wilford is going to prison for boys he abused."
In a tight voice, direct with concern Dad asks,
"Did that happen to you?"
I'm unmasked!
With a fearful long pause I reply,
"Yes."
Dad Knows.

III
I swim a roaring sea of confusion.
Heavy doses of shame, guilt overwhelm.
I anticipate Dad's anger, blame.

Terrified eyes burn with tears.
I can't speak.
He doesn't yell.
He doesn't hit.
We don't even sit.
No invitation to talk,
go for a walk...Nothing!
My father walks away.

What happens next I do not know
except I remember I have no memory.

Predator Wilford was caught
in terrible acts with other boys.
Under that fateful Tree,
he did to them what he did to me,
snared us with camp and boat,

used us as toys.
Unfinished pine board smell never leaves.

Even petunia's fragrance
can't disinfect that pine smell.
It "hangs" in my brain.

I get distorted "love" from a sick, criminal man,
instead of supportive, understanding father-love.
Ignoble silence is my father's fated, painful "gift."
Without supportive, caring words from Dad,
I imagine I am "mightily wrong," "very, very bad."
His silence drives me the rest of my life.

34

Next Stop!

A half-empty monastery near Bear Mt. Bridge
offers respite to hikers coming off
the Connecticut ridge.
Another place to rest, reflect, revisit my "pack,"
prepare to cross mighty Hudson River.

The River cuts deep,
a powerful, trauma-like "hope gift"
through the great Appalachian range;
points toward necessary drama,
for my life to hike into change.

Silent the Shadow.
Wide wings soar
high overhead.
No time to see
this graceful intermediary
float high in the sky.
Bright Sun blurs
my walking shadow-gift.
Hawk's momentary presence passes.
I am blessed!

35

Synchronicity--Blue Blaze

Morning sky is beautifully blue.
I wake anxious, angry,
as if this morning is too good to be true.

I prepare to walk with Pilar
the old Keene-to-Troy railroad track.
I can't seem to shake troubling feelings
as I strap on my little red fanny pack.

Outside, I discover last night's strong winds
dropped a big maple branch atop the woodshed.
Unseen above maple's leaves
Crow caws as it flies concerned around trees.

I walk down the track, Crow gifts a feather.
Hawk gifts another to this morning's feather collection.
Crow's feather sends me to Mt. Katahdin when Crow said:

"Get up! Get walking!
You have nothing to dread."

The branch fell gently.
No damage perpetrated the woodshed.
I carry on with uplifted emotions instead.
Not every found feather is a mystical gift.
Some finds simply remind: "Be kind."

PART III: UNPROTECTED

36

Between Two Rivers

I.
Over Bear Mountain Bridge, through the zoo,
up Bear Mountain I go,
following white blazes to high rocky places,
till Thundah, Stick, and I,
find sleeping spots among rocks
in "soft-enough" spaces.

Bear Mt. is lowest elevation,
oldest AT section.
Bear Mountain's lack of height
compensates
with hope, opportunity, wisdom, delight.

Hudson River is on the right.
Delaware is on the left.
Two hundred trail miles stretch south
provide monuments to history,
people to encounter, stories to remember,
odd places to rest...and more.
This earth space is a crucible,
a wonderful place to explore.

II.
I wake in fog's moist grey light.
A mysterious veil hides nascent messages from sight.
Experience reveals avenues to inner goodness.
Attention shifts inward.
Soul space glides when dark thoughts
slide to my darker side
where three dreams
shadow happenings not so bright.

37

Three New Dreams

1. Near NYC an airplane went crashing...

2. David stood nude before God dancing...

3. Jesus hung yelling from a tree:

   "Why have you forsaken me!"

IV.
Last night's dream reflections are short lived.
Restlessness breaks open edgy readiness.
Morning grey
air reeks with trouble.
Deep tension tightens the way water
twists and squizzels
when washing, wringing out
sweaty hiking shirts.
I would need a different kind of inner direction,
emotional protection to wash dirt
from this on-coming crucible
collection of greedy deception.

Clouds separate just enough to see
Hawk's shadow pass over trees.
Its broad wings spread,
awaken wide to morning sleepiness,
to frightful trouble ahead.

Hawk messenger, says: "Stick with it!
Trust your intuition, expand vision.
Fear is a prism, not a prison.
Fear shapes knowledge into wisdom!"

V.
Trail grapevine news reports,
a thief hides amidst trailside trees.
Some "Judas" stole a hiker's sacred cup,
leaves no way for him
morning rituals to conduct.
Hawk's cloudy morning "fly-over" reminds:
be aware,
seek larger vision.
This new age of Aquarius
we enter is very precarious.

Two days later without a sound
a north-bounder's pack
disappears in the middle of the night
right off its lean-to rack.
Left on the ground are only
a sly thief's sneaker tracks.

38

Three Trail News Items

Thundah's feet feel as if by lightning they'd been hit.
Pain is so bad, he almost quit.

Stick's upbeat positive attitude
gives a much-needed emotional lift,
reminds us of our underlying inner gifts.

My attention shifts;
A flashback occurs!
News of the AT thief,
poison ivy attack,
trigger long ago memories
of attacks by another kind of thief
as I walked my inner boyhood path.

I do not see the shiny three-leaf, oily poison hidden in
trail-side foliage and brush.
Poison scratches arm and knee,
penetrates skin,
forms excruciating itchy rash.

Poison ivy
reminds me of Wilford's sneaky, serpent touch!
Back then, he didn't seem dangerous or intent on harm.
Neither my parents nor I sounded the alarm.
This evil thief seduced permission
from Mom and Dad
with his well-disguised, clever "ask"
to take me for a ride in his shiny, slick Chris-Craft.
I took the ride.

39

Painful Discovery

I.
Walking between two rivers
during this mighty, mid-life journey,
I discover a wounded inner boy
full with trauma
walking his path with me.

The AT thief's poison ivy swipe
is contiguous like the path I hike
braids memories
steals purity of boyhood virginity,
triggers powerful manhood emotions
my inner boy does not understand.
I lost my sexual innocence!
Wilford's poison wounded this soul
never to be spoken of again
Shamed to silence,
I locked damaged boyhood feelings
in my inner closet
with other old abandonments
stored in my psychic trash bin.

II.
Is this what Hawk wants my eyes to recognize?
Is this what Hawk wants me to know:
use this melting pot between two rivers
to open doors shut long ago;
face pain, sorrow, dig deeper,
don't give up, restore myself?

Dream news
awakens this "flashback,"
invites healing,
leads inner boy to self-forgive,
frees Your love that
does not hold captive.

40

Healing Angel

Wawayanda Shelter is our stop this night.
No antidote do I carry in my pack,
for the blooming, poisonous plant.
I sit on a stump, clean the itchy wound
with boiled bottled water.
A "winged" woman hiker appears.
We greet each other.
With knowing concerned kindness she inquires:
"Do you know about jewel-weed?"
"No," I reply.

Off she "flies" with Hawk's speed,
returns "posthaste" with a handful of jewel-weed.
I am her student as she explains
poison ivy's healing opposite, jewel-weed.
She instructs how to us it
Quick as she arrived, she flies away.
This healing angel leaves me
a big fat jewel-weed poultice
to place on my skin,
wait for Mother Nature's healing to begin.

All kinds of wet: rain, fog, damp,
muddy our path, clothes, bodies,
make 6 days difficult to hike, to camp.
I wonder in my fantasy:
"Did We Three miss the Ark?"

7th morning comes.
Sun appears behind puffy white clouds
illuminating Earth's great amphitheater.
A musical orchestra of feathered instruments fills the air.
Around us melodious sonnets tweet, trill without a care.

Light honeysuckle aroma refreshes last night's heavy air.
Splashes of blue wave gently in field-grass as we pass.
Jacks in their pulpits plead for healing, peace.

Crow's caw for hope is unsurpassed.
Sounds of music through the forest
deepen as nearby geese honk
sounds of spring off into air.
I see clear horizon.
Exclaim my joy right out loud!
"I let go of something!"
"I receive something!"
Before You David danced,
I will not Die in Denia! I dance with a filling heart.
Your presence is not by chance.

41

The "Red Blaze"

Pain harms
Pain heals

Having eyes to see
ears to hear
skin to feel
poison ivy trauma pain
creates maps of connection
through soma, psyche, spirit
into brain for reflection

Skin is a personal organ
    defines who I am
    sets boundaries
    tells the world who I am
Skin is vulnerable
    can be broken
Skin can heal together again

Poison ivy attacked my skin
    touched my skin
    violated my skin

toxified my skin
with flashback trauma
harming my whole being

Trauma represses memory
disorders emotions
is insidiously seductive
impairs identity
Trauma generates electric
internal brain-body
system maps
Trauma pain sticks like glue
turning brain BLAZE RED!

Red Blaze has power
Red Blaze heals
Red Blaze says
don't isolate-communicate
do little things first
care for yourself
listen to music
meditate-celebrate

Red Blaze says
write *Hike to Alive*
walk the AT

Years have gone by.
Live Alive

Not in Denia, not anywhere else:
I have not Died.

Red Blaze pathway is
    contiguous
    guides through Age of Aquarius
Red Blaze transforms
    red pain into
    healing red blood energy
    as I twice hike the AT
    into this restorative,
    healing, contiguous tale!

42

Running

Running go my feet
driven by emotional pain
anger, fear, inadequacy, especially shame!

Memories chase me
through adolescence into adulthood.
I run through star-studded
high school and college athletics;
through lower and higher education
to ministry's Call: "Care for others."
Running becomes my life station.
When I'm too filled with shame,
to help myself with a life of pain,

I run in and out of two marriages,
through two courts of law
forcing me my sons to abandon.
I run to three
respected psychotherapists,
begin to trust them with shame I experience.

Each "fires" me,
leaves me abandoned under the "Tree"
with more shame.

43

Lost and Found

North Star flames like a rocket,
  points direction in middle of Night.
Mountain ranges, valleys, lakes, streams
appear in my dreams,
coax me out of fright.

One day Thundah and I, our wires did cross.
From on high we walk
an unmarked trail
a mile *down.*
We are lost!

Stand still!
Turn around.
Look at the ground.
Look at the trees.

I come to AT deeply lost.
Thundah is my witness.
North Star dream points the way.
Even in midday
suddenly, I find myself found!

Between rivers of Hudson and Delaware
lost in unconscious obsessiveness
with pain and shame too great to bear,
at that old cold road's end,
I wake up!

Mother Nature's beauty, wonder, heal!
In lostness I begin to turn my life around.
Lost? look to North Star.
"Knock, the door will open.
I sought. I'm found."

44

Inner Change

Inner change dreams itself to consciousness,
slowly opens like a chrysalis.

Simple natural elements
of mountains, fields, streams
soften soul seeds
planted long ago in dreams.

Earth's sacred soils unlock
God's beauty, wonder, mystery.

From inner soils
of chrysalis to midlife
I unveil slowly
the person I yearn to be.

45

Pain Meets Fate

Fate meets me. I meet fate.
We climb through the broken gate.
Hidden grief becomes alive.
Unknown loss is found.

Silently,
I carry forward
now known grief of three generations
of grandfathers and grandmothers.

Born into me is their pain,
an emotional scream,
like a fisher cat's scream
screeching in my soul.

Pain, hard like a stone at the gate,
lives in my heart, my brain
waits for the Rose
to walk with fate beyond the gate.

46

Preparation for Dragon's Teeth

High Point Mountain's top
sets a rocky ridge line on her open shoulder.
Panoramic New Jersey landscape
triggers wonder, wedding deepening vision:
"large without" with "large within."
Through fields of rocks and stones
I carry this vision, yet wonder:
"Can I walk into Dragon's mouth of jagged teeth?"

The prophet Micah answered:
"What does the Lord require of you?
Walk humbly with your God?" (Micah 6:8)

Crow offers encouragement, support,
leaves a shiny black wing feather
beside the trail.
The gift is gracious.
My spirits lift.

Micah's words echo:
"Keep walking, be humble,
even if you stumble,
trust reminders,
'You can do this.' "

I face fear.
Crow takes fear.
I walk toward Dragon's Teeth,
embrace pain as a gift.
Broken parts are planted
to grow in soil of my soul.
Yes. I can do this.

47

Rebecca's Inn

Thundah's friend Rebecca,
knows we're coming through,
offers an overnight stop,
gives generous hospitality
to "we three kings"
before we take on Pennsylvania Rocks.

Warm-hearted, magnanimous Becca
meets us at the designated spot.
Three smelly men into her car hop,
dirty up clean seats,
jam three dirty packs into the trunk.
Off she speeds us to shower, meal, bunk.
We sleep between sweet-smelling sheets.

Table mounds of food,
highlights with tasty chicken fricassee.
Glasses of wine lift with grace.
We share stories, tell tales
laced with fun-loving, hale-hearty faces.

A comfortable bed, a good night's rest,

juice, coffee, bacon aplenty, eggs for breakfast,
Becca speeds thankful guests back to the AT,
With hugs and well wishes:
"Thank you, Becca! You're a friend at its best.
God bless!"

48

"Rocksylvania" PA

Round rocks, sharp rocks, rocks loose and jagged
stick up in every direction, to make my body haggard.
Pointy rocks sting, pain, jab,
make scratches, bumps, bruises
turn into annoying scabs.

Rocks challenge my body
from head to toe, to soul.
I carefully place my feet
avoid bites from dragon's teeth.

The footpath determines gait
whether my feet go fast or slow.
I spread my legs wide for stability.
Still, my Limmer's are liability.
These fine boots don't enhance my usual agility.
My feet swim in unexpected painful uncertainty.

The hike through "Rocksylvania" is like trauma
trying to heal wounds that will not heal.
We traverse blistering rocks for 100 miles.
Ankles turn, slip, pain.

Heel blisters weep, weep some more.
"How much hurt must I endure?"

My body tells me:
Slow down, move along
make room,
for a meditative "Shadow Walk."
Let pain guide healing

49

"No Room at the Inn"

At Kirkridge Retreat Center a restful night we anticipate.
Rock "Teeth" take us along a bordering stone wall
to "Administration" where we expect
overnight information.

"No Room at the inn. Boy Scouts on retreat,"
the sign says...
No rest for our tired bodies, blistering feet.
We must search for a smooth rock-bed.

Back to White Blazes, tired, wobbly steps
lead to young hardwoods.
Off in the dusk I see
clumps of grass, weeds.
Without a word: I enter the grove right.
Thundah enters left.
Stick keeps searching.

I find two long parallel stones
lying along the ground
reminiscent of knife edge granite chunks.
I choose this spot.

Between serrated stone edges,
the mattress I wedge.

The sight through trees above comforts me.
Milky Way mixes black and white.
Rainbow color explodes across the sky,
softens rocks on which I lie.
I uncomfortably sleep.

50

Breath

Breathe in. Breathe out.
Strict attention draws careful step selection,
walking with focused intention,
on AT's hardest section.

Morning sunlight works its way
through morning haze.
Body warms with goodness.
I lift my gaze.
A long emergent shadow
my "hiker shape" displays!

Soul splits open
the way seeds hiding in dark places split open
when suddenly they come to light.

I gasp!
Breathe in. Breathe out.
Don't talk.

Inner Wisdom speaks:
"Press on!
Confront Great Mystery.
Shadow walk."

51

Shadow Walk

I.
Crow knows:
Shadow Walk is a great mystery!
combines black and white,
creates rainbow color,
lights up Milky Way
in the middle of night.

Crow knows:
In Milky Way darkness
Moon's long Shadow
hides buried treasure.
Constrains dark
lights up star dots,
to reveal rainbow colors.

Crow knows:
I'm conceived in darkness,
born innocent with my Shadow,alone.
At 3 Dad held me to black night window:
"Look at the full moon on the river."

I see "giant" Sturgeon
arch up through full Moon reflection
splash down
in moon's river Shadow
to underwater dark.

Crow knows:
Shadow carries past hurts,
hides generational wounds
in over and under water cycles,
turns soul to stone,
blinds becoming whole.

Crow knows:
Shadow masks, splits off,
unknown, unseen
broken parts of heart and soul,
veils them in the dark.

Crow knows: Treasure is discovered in darkness.
Golden riches wait in secret places.
Hidden gold found in death's valley of shadows
shapes identity,
creates wholeness.

II.
Crow guides:
Rainbow light beams
to soul wounds that refuse to heal.
Illuminates wounds in inner spaces
bringing freedom's trail to new life.

Crow's Caw Caw Caw guide:
"Medicine Bird," take him to the wound.
Root out evil!
Look the Devil in the eye.
Confront the devil bastard!
Cast out the pedophiliac!

Open doors to ancestor wounds.
directs shining light to this
lifelong healing path
splashing from Kennebec's
Moon-lit Shadow's treasure.

Crow guides:
Sun's white light
to star stories behind night's black veil.
I watch ancient night sky tales travel,
connect dots with Ancient Earth stories.
I cry!
North Star of my soul,
in tears hope arises.

III.
Crow Reminds:
"I am a creature of here and there.
Black feathers of Rainbow color
in my wings,
I carry through the air.

Year after year for nine,
I light your journey.

Drop a feather on the trail,
bring wonder to Shadow misery
you carry.

Crow Reminds:
Keep trudging the AT!
It's a treasure chest of riches.
Open it! Shadow walk. I fly with you
over mountain tops, in ditches.
"You are not alone."

52

Burial Ground

We stand a silent trinity,
among grave markers,
trees in an ancient burial ground
where stories of slaves and
indigenous Americans abound.

Earth is alive!
Silent drums move my feet
pulsing
a felt heartbeat.

Songbirds
flute a musical chorus
of "Welcome" for us.
Large birds
draw spirals in the sky
as on this sacred path we pass by.

Markers and stones drummed by bones
give life, identity, hold meaning,
tell stories of that one particular person,
risen beyond the grave,

who lives on through sacred memory.
Red Rainbow color rises
from blood of the ancients.
Voices of the dead
bleed from six-pointed stars.
Grave markers
speak from stone Buddhas, crosses,
carved stone feather wreaths.

No matter the burial,
a person's color,
black, brown, red, white,
life lives here!

Living stories remain,
connect ancient tales,
of those who have gone before,
with we three who pass by now.

53

Bowl of My Soul

I.
I walk cheerful through woods,
glad to leave rocks behind.
Virginia AT path greets me,
leads me with gentle mind
toward Garden Mountain's round summit
at this difficult incline.

Sun blesses,
surrounds Earth with warmth.
Forest floor wiggles
with life seen and unseen.
Snake slithers through leaves.
I listen to bees.
Friends are trees.
Land is heart's beat,
Earth's the drum.
This is healing medicine.

I round a corner to the summit.
What an unexpected sight I see!
"God's Thumbprint!"

Garden Mountain creates
a bowl in an ancient sea,
Burke's Garden below,
creates "Bowl of Soul!"

II.
This Bowl-like crucible
contains more
than I can ever imagine,
more than I'll ever know!
Down there,
patchwork farms dot landscape like a quilt.

Tree lines, street lines, stream lines,
roof lines, clothes lines, power lines,
charge soul's energy lines.

I hear a story about Varmint of Burke's Garden,
a lone coyote, who kills lambs and sheep
causing great damage,
shepherds not to sleep.

Here, I invite ancestors to walk with me,
support my soul confrontation
with the "evil coyote" thief
who ravaged, stole innocence,
left me alone with grief.

III

I stand encircled by Garden Mountain's summit.
I see life expand beyond Shadow.
Between tree groves, vegetable gardens,
peaceful cows safely graze
in pastures green, lazy.

I see the "sacred circle" below
where trees, leaves, grasses invite healing;
where sky, earth, air, renew life;
where water, fire, spirit, silence, mix
heal brokenness.

Everything wants to be "round."
Spirit, body, mind
want to round toward wholeness.

In this round Temple of Nature,
truth, freedom awaken.
Trust beckons.
Hope is alive.
Love is energized.

54

Half-Way: Pine Grove Furnace, PA

I.
Overhead leaf canopy
arches as cathedrals arch
to create sunspots of sanctuary light
across an altar rail.

Ahead, I see the halfway point,
a blazed post with splotches of paint
splashed opposite each other as if to anoint
this spot.

Two arrows point in opposing directions:
one points North. The other points south.
North pointer reads: Mt. Katahdin-1,069 miles.
South pointer reads: Springer Mt.- 1,069 miles.
Atop the post, AT logo reads:
APPALACHIAN TRAIL- MAINE TO GEORGIA.
I'm going to Georgia!

II.
At the post, I stop in my tracks,
slide my pack to the ground,
Step back...Listen to silent sounds.
Reflect:
Six years! Laughter, tears,
over many a mountain-top trekking,
through many a fence gate climbing,
under, over several stone bridges
along pleasant ridges.

Midway to Georgia
with Stick and Thundah,
I stand in noble silence,
unite this midlife journey walk
with inner reflection, physical trekking,
Star-filled skies, fields full of flowers
increasing confident nobility.

Year after year Crow persists,
insists I overcome doubt.
Medicine Bird Crow
leaves another feather, trailside gift saying:
"Don't resist. Accept possibility.
Let go of fear.
Trust what you know, you know.
Caw! Caw!
Trust what you know you know."

This Sacred Journey
embeds itself
in creation's crucible of Sacred Mystery,

embeds itself
in personal history.

III.
Memory of sacred Sturgeon
jumps from Kennebec's full-moon center,
speaks from mountains, Katahdin, Agiocochook,
to God's Thumbprint.
Memory makes
childhood experience real again,
opens treasure chest to Great Mystery.
I can't explain why it's so.
I Know. I feel whole.

One thousand sixty-nine miles to go!

PART IV:
HEALING
CONSCIOUSNESS

55

Great Smokies

My "just before dawn" tracks stop
to watch a powerful golden glow
stretch across the sky
from horizon to horizon.
Sun's light gift
guides AT hikers.
All we have to do
is receive.
Two white-blazed, weather-beaten posts
frame "Cosmic Artist's"
exquisite, intensely natural palate.

Distant Smoky Mountain Ridges
appear as Asian tapestry.
Golden threads
catch every molecule of sunlight,
undulate,
twinkle gold.

Each blade of foreground grass shines.
I'm a fleeting shadow,
here today, gone tomorrow;

yet golden strands glitter around me,
invite eternal wonder,
offer newness now!
I step into the picture frame.
A magic carpet seats me,
lifts me to sky.
Below, the sacred path
unwinds like a spool of thread
through Great Smoky Mountain air.
A breeze softly blows.
Bathed in gold,
down this golden trail, I slowly go.

56

Pilar

O Honeysuckle
sweet, sweet ambrosia of Spring,
your fragrant perfume
softly finds its way to my nostrils.
I wake!

O sweet, my sweetheart, Pilar,
flower of Spring,
your honeysuckle fragrance
effervesces,
embraces senses.
My heart sings!

57

Two "Feathahs"

The path's middle,
offers Thundah a Crow Feathah.
With reverence
Thundah places it in my hand.

Later, trailside,
Crow releases
a second feather.
I place this Feathah gift
in Thundah's hand.

"Trail Magic" exchange,
blends Crow's grace, God's grace.

Hiking the AT,
ineffable, inner space
spirals!

Poem written, signed, sent June 2022.
A Crow wing Feathah was included.

58

Harpers Ferry

"Feathah" rang out a voice
from the iron bridge structure.

Son-in-law, Antonio,
camera in hand,
snaps a picture
as I walk under the bridge
toward Harpers Ferry.

Antonio arrives from D.C.,
Brings lunch.
Passes me a card
from his mother, Pilar.

We sit,
sun on river's grassy bank,
eat slices of prosciutto and brie,
munch apples, dried fruit, cookies.
Drink ample amounts of delicious iced tea.

"Trail Angels," like feathers,
float in from the air.

Proffer generous gifts,
offer encouragement, inspiration
to continue walking
through arenas of great history,
present synchronicity.

59

"Wanted"

I.
A buzzard circles overhead.
Poison ivy lines the path.
Sunning Snake rattles
from a nearby rock, warns of danger ahead.

A park ranger appears.
I tell him about the "weird guy"
at Crampton Shelter
who felt like
a dangerous rattler in the grass.
Ranger pulls a paper from his pack.

WANTED BY FBI, reads the poster.
"Eric Rudolph is charged
with bombing an abortion clinic
in Birmingham, Alabama,
critically wounding a nurse,
killing a police officer."
A gun is known to be carried
by this evil monster.

Ranger hands out the "Wanted" poster.
Says "Stay far away from him,
as far as you can."

II.
Another devil-snake monster
hides in the woods.
In my skin I shake!
Threat of poisonous Snake,
murderer Rudolph,
triggers flashback fear, rekindles uncertainty.
Trauma flashbacks come in many forms, even death.
Stop, they do not!

A dark Shadow forms across my path.
I hear distant thunder play warning drums.
Storm is on the way.

Whippoorwill sings, brook babbles.
Snake Back Trail
defines Virginia-West Virginia state line.

III.
The storm didn't arrive.
Shenandoah Valley 3,000-footers lift the horizon.
Crow caws in the distance.
Nature's Cathedral softens my fear,
lightens raw Shadow power.
I walk steady, quicker than usual, make good time.

60

Trillium Rhythm

I.
I walk slow this morning.
New moods fill my body.
Dreams, meditations
signal new clues.

Bird flute sounds
Crescendo, erupt
rise symphonic,
like pure Trillium white
combining brilliant, bright
across the forest garden floor.

Animal melody voices unite,
open doors to this shining Trillium light.
Dark Shadow notes diminish.
I leave them swinging behind open doors.
There will always be ashes and residue,
as I pan for gold to accomplish the new.

This morning,
my heart plays golden rhythm.

Joy blends temperament,
through intervals of dark and light.
Wide awake, I hike.

II.
I look down forest avenue
lined with tall slender trees.
They bend and bow
touch each other with leaves
like contra dancers bend and bow
as their dance-floor lines allow.

Body rhythms open my "dance."
Subtle, fragrant aroma
stirs my senses.
Dance floor expands.
I swing, sway with forestial music.
With musical movement
Spirit, breath, body dance with wind
amidst this dazzling display of white Trillium.
I am alive! My pack turns light!

61

Mountain Laurel

I.
It's Spring!
Life outside sprouts anew!
Inner seeds spring anew!
Renewal is all around!

I poke, push, pull
from inside my cocoon
till I break out,
see the full silver moon!

I am that miracle.
The world's natural beauty
tells me so.
Its allegorical!
Early morning haze moistens my gaze.
Mountain Laurel tunnel before my eyes opens.

I cry!
Beautiful Blue Ridge Mountains
invite interplay of dark and light.
In this floral Laurel forest

I walk without talking,
listen as soft breezes
play black and white piano keys,
make music on leaves,
through speckled sunlight.

II.
I move under deep, dense arches
of blooming laurel clusters,
with their tiny teacups,
of red, pink, white.

No one is worthy,
to drink from these
elegant tiny teacups
dotted with innocent pinheads,
tiny black dots.
Beauty seduces, tempts, masks
deadly poison held by these cups.

I dance tightrope tension.
Floral beauty peril prempts
as I search amidst light and dark Shadows.
Each step I take offers possibility
to balance healing
without drinking poison tea.

62

Gravel Springs Shelter

Shelter is full this foggy night.
I am spent!
Everything is damp.
The world is wet tonight.

Hikers gather at the picnic table,
turn it into a communion table.
Bread shared. Cup drunk. Stories told.
Communion happens here.

Hikers crawl into their sleeping bags.
The "Altar" is my bed.
I Pull the tarp over my head.
Fold a jacket into a pillow.
Tonight, I'm out like a light.

I wake in middle of night,
realize this "Altar"
is sacred space.
Clouds disappear.
Heavens are crystal clear.

Milky Way blesses,
spreads light everywhere.

I look up in awe.
Millions, billions of stars,
see into my eyes.
My heart trembles.
"Far" is "near."
Psalmists proclaim their glory!
Poets sing, write heaven's story!
Mercurial mystery touches my soul!

63

Mac, The Widower--Blue Blaze

I sit at "Georgia Mountain Restaurant Bar."
Uninvited, the sloppy old man
wobbles over,
sits beside me.

"I'm Mac Moore, trail angel."
"What's your trail name?"
"Crow Feathah."

"I heard you talkin to the bartendah:
I can take you to the PO, the grocery store,
then to my house.
While you take a shower,
I'll wash your clothes."

Immediate suspicions!
This "too nice" scruffy old man
touches off trauma flashback
memories for me.

My body stiffens.
Defensive mode quickens.

I glance for assurance
from the bartender,
who nods, "He's OK."

Mac reminds me of "Commish,"
a Boy Scout leader I did trust.
I cautiously take the risk.

Down the road we go,
made the stops.
Mac begins to talk.
"I'm 80. My wife of fifty-two years
died six years ago."

Like a broken dam
Mac's grief pours out,
a stream of tears
He gives words to sorrow.
I listen.

"Sorry, my house is such a mess.
I don't cook, I don't clean,
She took care of all that stress."

"I'm an active Boy Scout leader.
Mt. Rainey Boy Scout Camp
is a few miles down the road.
There's a banquet tonight,
a new dining hall dedication.
I want to take you there for dinner,

to join our celebration.
My grief load lightens.

Such events distract.
Mac is a true Trail Angel.
I imagine every lonely night
Mac envisions his wife
before he sleeps and dreams.
At waking, he wipes his eyes
pulls on his pack
of unbearable loneliness and grief.

Morning comes.
To the Restaurant Bar he drives,
spreads his wings of compassion,
supports, encourages hikers
as we travel through these
healing Appalachians.

64

Color Guard

Ups and downs undulate like an inchworm
in this 300-mile section.
Trail offers pause, time for reflection.
My feet fall smooth.
Great Smokies and Virginia Ridge Blues
set canvas for artist's brush, poet's pen,
singer's song.

White wild roses bend, bloom
along a pasture fence,
waft gentle aroma to morning air.
Rose fragrance blends,
with snapdragon's breath,
mixes, smells sweet and fair.

Light blue dwarf iris' embrace,
a Civil War soldier monument.
Long silent guns blaze.
Bloody tales of shot up, torn up
Blue-grey-coated bodies,
men, women who fought, died for freedom
are memorialized along this part of the trail.

Orange daylilies appear.
Stamens, honor guard of the patch,
stand tall at high attention.
Sight, color, aroma fuse
into spiritus beauty,
as these flowers yearly honor fallen warriors,
acknowledge sacrifice,
remind "liberty and justice are for all."
I celebrate life's freedom for all
on this planet, and for me!

65

Catawba Rhododendron

I.
I leave darkened valleys of death Shadow trauma.
I don't feel squeezed by evil's grip any longer.
Along the Tennessee/North Carolina state line,
Catawba Rhododendron spectacular gardens
rise high into sky, beautify my mind.

Roan Bald's wide grassy spaces
push a button,
release me!
My inner boy skips
through the grass!

Soul seeds planted long ago
Break-out, grow!
Night starlight touches, unites earth flower light.
Grief softens. Up here the path "in" opens.
Vistas of wonder display Fields of Dreams.

II.
I shadow-walk Your magnificent cathedral highlands
amidst rhododendron purple-magenta wisdom,

red-orange flame azalea.
I carefully place my feet.
Shadow and Spirit meet.
Flower vistas,
Mountaintop ridges, palettes of color
send me somewhere off in air
floating between bright Earth and Night Sky.

If I Die in Denia, don't bury me there!

66

Mother Earth

I.
Without darkness
     no spring.

Without worms
     no flowers.

Fallen leaves
     decompose.

Sunlight warms Earth,
     seeds sprout
     new trees to birth.

II.
Step after step,
     two souls
     walk outer landscapes.

Morning after morning after morning,
     dream talk sharing
     guides through labyrinth landscapes.

Light breaks open truth,
     stretches toward the sun,
     exposes "gold."

"Gold" mixes with "Dark."
     dream-time inscape
     illumines, contiguous trails.
     Inner life grows.

67
Salty Dog

I.
Sun is hot.
Humidity is high.
Lots of sweat.
Shirts, shorts, socks
are soaking wet.

Shelter is quiet.
No one here yet.
Thundah and I strip.
Hang our "wets" on a branch
to give them a chance to air-dry.

II.
Deer-quiet Doe steps
out of the woods.
Her movement catches our eyes.
We stand still.

Doe goes directly to Thundah's shirt.
Gathers into her mouth
sweaty shorts, socks, shirt,

chews-licks-sucks-shakes salt
right out from these sweaty threads.

III.
I laugh quietly. Thundah does too.
Doe doesn't scare.
She chews his shirt beyond repair.

To Thundah I whisper playfully, "It's OK"
 Doe seems to say:

"'You are salt of the earth'
Do you mind if I have a lick,
replenish my salt today?" (Matthew 5:13-16)

I savor the playful salty experience.
It gives me a kick.
I tuck it away in my mindful memory stick.

68

Nap on a Log

Once, Ancient American Chestnut trees
grew from small seeds,
foresting Great Smoky Mountain flanks
with homes for myriad of plants, animals, humans, trees
to live, breed, give thanks.

The "blight" came in twenty-five,
decimated these towering trees.
Killed the giants. None remain alive.
They died, fell in great criss-cross patterns
spread over the wooden bone graveyard
like an old patchwork quilt tattered and torn.

I find my "nap-time" bed,
a fallencomfortable, wide trunk,
on a great, long-deceased
American Chestnut tree.

I lie on the log,
pull the quilt over me,
peek out from under the cover,

see life, death, clear blue sky.
I breathe wonder.

"In fifteen years how in the world
could a few invasive Asian molecules
blight, kill this ancient forest
this tree?"

No answer came, only tears of protest!
"How could hands of a sexually invasive man
abuse a ten-year-old boy,
wound his soul for the rest of his years!"

Such memories tire me out!
They come because
the "veil" is torn.
Seeing beyond the veil
helps me be reborn.
I Am Not Dead!
I hide my eyes under the quilt.
Settle my soul, take a nap.
I will heal.

69

Overnight Blue Blaze

"FreeMan" arrives at the shelter near dusk.
Backpacking guitar protrudes from his pack.
Blue bandana covers his head.
Silver-rimmed oculars hang over his eyes.
Beard darkens his face.
Is this John Lennon dropping in from outer space?

Our Trinity shares leftovers.
Storytelling begins.
Emotional energy, spiritual conversation
reveal inner similarities
of our midlife transformations.

Everyday life has eternal rhythms.
Music echoes of
death and discovery,
healing and recovery,
skies above, earth below,
hearts within.

New rhythms pulse my heart.
Evening melodies awaken.

Immediate is our 4-way connection.
Trinity welcomes the medicine doc.
Midlife journeys
are now quarternity.

70

FreeMan's House, VA

Four years later:
I sit see FreeMan across the table.
Blue bandana covers his head.
Gold-rim glasses oculars cover his eyes.
Face bearded as if to disguise.

Fuzzy, soft dark hair covers baby Andrew's head.
Tiny pensive eyes,
Round face, cute smile
Bring smiles to my face.

Cuddled, held by proud Harriet
baby Andrew is a cute whipper-snapper,
as he readies for his afternoon napper.
FreeMan's arms embrace
family with warmth like a blanket wrapper.

Father, son look off in wonder.
Dad's restrained smile
holds back pride.
Mom's warm smile radiates.
My heart bursts out with a shout!

They are Father and Son
I see Father in Son.
I see Son in Father.

Through them, I see me,
recall play with Dad
on the living room rug when I was three.
Who will this father, son become?

A Trinity fed a hungry man at dusk.
Like the trail
another Trinity feeds us
enriches, nourishes memory,
feeds soul and body on our journey.

71

Somehow

Here:
I gaze into blue curling haze rivers.
Fluffy, goose-down feathers gather in clouds.
Above haze, Crow "Caw, Caw!"

Somehow:
In these high mountains,
a boyhood memory of wild geese
flies to my mind in a "V."

North up Kennebec River geese speak,
pleasant honking memories
from the Memory Giver.

I hike South to fly North,
swim in soul-healing waters.
This old memory is new.

Up here, I reach past words.
My arms, like wings, open.
Unique Peace awakens.

PART V: CREATION'S WISDOM

72

Dog's Leg

I.
In woods hiking up Big Bald,
Thundah takes a bad bump, thump
on his forehead.
Falls!
Path footing is easy.
His eyes play tricks.
He doesn't see a branch overhang.
The blast puts him on his ass.

Rest, water, food get him
back on his shaky feet.
He'll need both legs,
a clear head,
to finish this next-to-last leg.

II.
A lost dog found Thundah!
What an unimaginable find
for the dog, for Thundah.
His bump softens, His spirits pick up.

He's a hiker,
knew he would get through.

Dog is scared, hungry,
wiggly, very friendly
needs attention.
Like an aspirin, relieves pain,
Thundah is distracted.
His load lightens through this rough moment.
Gives him time to recharge, reload.

The abandoned critter
hikes with us for 15 miles.
We meet shuttle driver Miss Janet,
at Nolichucky River.
Her sister works for a vet.
Off the dog goes to a caring place,
a story we will never forget.

73

Tell Me

O Mountain Laurel
    Tell me:

Do you reflect
    night sky stars?

Do you receive
    skylight brightness
    in star-cup blooms?

How is starry night sky
    transformed
    sparkly white?

I embrace Creation's embrace.

74

Healing Place

Every year,
I walk the next section.
Space out here
is safe.
There's ample time for reflection.

Nature embraces soul wounds.
in hidden places where
stars bump and thump
into each other
form new stars.
Emotional, spiritual scabs
fall off inexplicably.

Is this not where God lives?
Sparkling among star Shadow seeds
deposited in "Garden of Youth" spaces
when light and dark bump?
Gold grows slow in the soul.

Today,
air is fresh, sweet.

Honeysuckle scent seeps,
fills senses with nectar of grace,
as hummingbird draws
droplets of golden sweet hope
through its beak.

Every year,
I walk Earth-trail space.
Every year
I move deeper and deeper
toward inspired healing victory.
God does not give up.
Soul receives wings, Crow's Caw.
By God's ineffable, affectional magnitude, (love)
I am embraced.

75

Thundah's Slowing

Thundah begins to slow down.
Space along the ground,
stretches out between us.
He says his legs ache feet burn.
I see his weeping blisters squirm.
This is no laughing matter.

Thunder booms. Rain falls.
Thundah Booms!!!
"I can do this! I can do this!
I'll slow down! I'll rest!
This last section, I'll finish!"

We slow down. Hide from rain.
Thunder passes.
We take more stops.
Give time for muscles, cells, tissues,
to coordinate, balance, gain strength,
let his feet have more needed rest breaks.

We speak:
"We journey together a sacred pilgrimage.

Blessings we experience.
Pain we endure amplifies our strides
34' and 38' motions forward,
of that we are sure."

Patiently, steps become
committed presentations,
of ourselves to incremental change
within ourselves, with each other, with God.

I witness Thundah's pilgrimage,
become clear: a focused
relationship with God.
Our pilgrimage, our journey
we do not want to short-change.

Excerpted from "Life at 2 miles an hour."
Denis T. Noonan, III

76

Slowing Down--Blue Blaze

I.

Back in Portland the Medical Report:
Thundah's hiking prognosis
for next year worsens.
Doctor's diagnoses
hold forth in his court:

"Deep-vein thrombosis,
with an added case of cellulitis.
Put your leg up. Rest.
No scratches, no bleeding,
slow down,
No more hiking this year!"
For a high-stepping AT section hiker
terrible news!

II.

Thundah works with his leg up
taking half the space on his desk.

"I can't function. I can't reach the phone.
My legs, my eyes tumble me into great distress!..

Life is full of wonderful inconsistencies,
challenging humor, known and unknown."

The landscape of Thundah's body cries out
For golden miracles.
Inscape yeans for hummingbird nectar
to be his personal remedy.
Gold_*is*_here.
Nectar *will* come.

Thundah listens:
Nature's healing wholeness guides.
Hope and disappointment mix.
He sits, till 2002;
Hides in Portland's fog.
Waits for Sun.

77

O My God!

I.
O my God!

Doc said:
"Don't go in '01!
Give your legs and feet a rest.
In '02 put them to the test!"

Terrible news!
Thundah and I never imagined this!
We're on track
to "finish" in '01.

My heart is broken.
It cracks. What will I do!
Will I or won't I go?
Awful decision!
Indecision means plan revision.
Do I finish in '01 or NO?

II.
Sometimes it takes a dynamite blast
to open a new mountain path:
like the one blasted through Appalachians
at Newfound Gap!

III.
I decide to go,
hike this last section solo.
The fuse lit.
Powerful emotions, anger, rage,
sadness, sorrow
mix between Thundah and Crow.
BOOM goes the blast!
CAW! CAW! cries Crow.

Our foundational connection,
rumbles, bends, bows,
booms, caws,
screams across mountaintops,
lights up the sky as if daylight!
Will our love,
our care stand such fury?

Patience, trust beget gentle grace,
for life's aliveness
to maintain a separate steady pace.
What is my task? What must I do?
The blast is a way through.

IV.
Descending Katahdin at journey's beginning,
I injured my knee,

took time out to heal, to rest.
Thundah moved onward.

Now, Thundah's legs and feet,
give out.
He needs time to heal, to rest.
I move onward.

Solo bookends,
hold our AT experience together.
Each of us hiked our first section solo.
Can each of us hike our last section solo,
cherish to integrate our growth-producing connection?

78

Black Horse Meditation

I dream,
I stand with Black Horse,
called to an enlarged different world,
of aging, initiation, transformation.

Suddenly,
Hawk's Shadow crosses my path!
Interrupts this morning's
walking meditation.

I ask:
"Feathered messenger of meaning,
What is my task?
What of me do you ask?"

Hawk's reply:
"Heed my message.
Listen to your dream.
Place your eyes,
in eyes of Black Horse."

I accept the invitation:
Crawl from under the table.
Climb upon Black Horse,
who takes me into sky,
away from dark fear,
painful abuse memories.

"Shadow wounds heal,"
says Black Horse.
"You can't hide.
Don't fool yourself by being less.
Time to take the next step."

79

Glimpse Toward Paradise

Black Horse eyes look into mine.
Stars bump. Paradise blooms
into an enlarged, different world
of aging, initiation, maturation;
sets a new trajectory arching toward death
into paradise.

I don't need to know
what heaven or life after death is like.
I do know the embrace of Earth's healing unity
is universal beauty.

Like Black Horse,
I seek space beyond the world I live in.
I stride solo
into forests of new time.
I am the path. The path is mine.

Some believe walking on water is a miracle.
To walk on earth is to walk
the sacred miracle inside me.

If I die in Denia, float my ashes
in Appalachian Mountain air,
where there is no death,
only fierce beauty and gratitude.
I'll live embraced by mystery there
in God's eternal breath.

80

Trail Markers

Alone,
    Together
    trust.
Stones
    Touch,
    Stacked up
Cairns
    Guide,.
    Encourage
    Lead
    to next white blaze.

No mother's arms reach,
    To touch, or strengthen,
    gather me to her side,
    To ease the pain.

No father's hand in mine
    Reassures,
    Rests on my shoulder.

I long for Sun
    Warmth,
    Embrace,
     to melt darkness.

Roll away the Stone,
heal,
feel mystery of empty space.
    Is this my destiny?

81

Laurel Creek Falls, TN

Laurel Creek Falls
spread the stream,
a pure-white wedding veil.

Mist shrouds Pilar,
perched on a rock
like Lilinoe,
goddess of mist.

On the bank down stream
into my soul mists Lilinoe
as though a dream.

82

Wesser Bald Mountain

On Wesser Bald,
I stand still,
mesmerized by
empty canvas underbelly
of Smoky Mountain haze.

One wide,
golden stroke after another,
the Cosmic Artist's brushstrokes
highlight
shepherds, cupids, angels, queens.
Ancient Gothic arches spread like seeds
Van Gogh's golds and greens
like God's seeds, before me.

My heart-drum beats.
Am I standing on the ceiling
or on the floor?

"Yes, You are here.
Your rod, staff and Crow
comfort me.

You anoint my head with oil.
My cup overflows.
Surely, goodness and mercy
will follow me,
all the days of my life."

PART VI: TRANSFORMATION

83

Seeing Beyond

Nine years in a row?
Crow bestows a "Feathah gift."
How do I understand this meaning?

Year 10:
Thundah healed, finished.
Crow gave him a feather gift.
Thundah gave that sacred 10th to me.
It's what "brothers" do.

When I meditate Thundah's gift,
Deep tears rise in my eyes.
Thundah knows years of traumatic sorrow
I carry inside.

He saw beyond healing moments:
ineffable joy in Vermont,
as rain poured, pounded our heads;
as intense rainbow color emerged,
from the trail in woods ahead.

Laughing Thundah witnessed me
"wash" in mud-blood of the AT
Birth a new Self, the person I am called to be.

Change happens.
My pack is light.
Thundah is my witness,
sees I carry hope and delight.

In a year,
Thundah will "Finish."
Celebration awaits
hot fudge sundaes,
tall frothy glasses of
Crow-black Guinness.

84

Pilar is Here

The seed is planted!
Mother Nature's Life-flow
pulses new within!
Emotional energy changes
when a spouse joins
like a plant changes
with too much or too little
morning sun's light.

Pilar is present
the way rising sun stirs
new life in morning coffee;
endows mind, body, soul.
Pilar joins five days for "The Finish."
Our strengths intermingle, rejuvenate.
I discover inner parts of myself
I do not know.

II
She accepts the invitation.
Steps begin.
I watch her every move,

quicken with excitement
amidst forest, flowers, plants.

Web of Life spins
from her Spanish ancestral cave.
Pilar cares for Earth
protects our planet,
as did her ancestors 30,000 years before.

Natural World beauty draws her sharp attention
to subtleties of color, shape, form.
"Little things" inspire "big things."
Her creativity web catches me,
invites seeing
how gentle hues emerge
from personal connection.

Her artistic inspiration,
rolls back my veneer,
unveils hiddenness.
Relationship shines.

When Pilar speaks,
Her eyes glisten.
I listen.
From her web of life,
Creation's glory freshens.
Inside, excitement quickens!
My Heart sings:
 "Joyful! Joyful! we adore thee. ...
Hearts unfold like flowers before thee."

("Ode to Joy," Friedrich Schiller, original author)

85

What Happened!

I.
The sign aged out, unreadable,
unpreserved by human care.
Object of neglect,
shelter disintegrated,
No place to rest.

Humans did to shelter,
what we do to the world around us:
Humans alienate hands that feed us.
We set ourselves high,
on hard-to-reach shelves.

II.
A southbound blue blaze
lifts us up the little hill's lip.
Strewn, charred wood
lies over the ground.
Here, we hoped to sleep tonight.
Not to be!
The broken shelter is fallen down.

"In those pines a fire circle you will find
a satisfactory place to sleep,"
said three north-bounders,
pointing toward forest deep.

Over and down the lip we go,
find this night's place.
Ambushed by Love,
this craftmanship is God's grace.
Tonight, we fellowship with
the great Artist in a geologic bowl.

The fire circle appears.
Several species of bushes, trees,
A few colorful, unknown wildflowers,
decorate the bowl with odd beauty.
I even hear bees.

A squirrel scurries,
pops an acorn into Earth to rot,
marks the spot.
A year later during his "finish"
Thundah finds the spot,
sees a tiny sprout,
shows the spot to his
wood turner-hiker-grandson.
The young fella sees the tree,
prunes a branch,
turns a fancy-lip wooden bowl.

By this dream story of
life, death, life
rising from the ash heap
Thundah is warmed with peace.

86

Dance of Goodbyes

I.
A bronze plaque
bolted to stone
holds the message:

"The Appalachian Trail is a footpath
for those who seek fellowship with the Wilderness."
Georgia Appalachian Mountain Trail Club, 1934.

From the plaque a bronze relief hiker
surges northward
toward Katahdin's summit.
He carries an old cloth backpack,
wears a '30s hat.

The rock I sit on
anchors me to sacred ground.
I journal-write, dedicate,
this last "go-round"
to objectified, traumatized,
sexual abuse victims.
May God's creation set your

your healing Homeward bound!

II
I enter wilderness,
summon Life's sacred ways
of fellowship, friendship, healing,
to transform brokenness into well being.
I dance homeward alive to renewed destiny.
Steps in the beginning were awkward.
I didn't know it.

Each Spring I continue to dance,
clean out infection,
disinfect troublesome behavior.
Through walking meditation,
meaningful conversation,
I discover how new steps,
summon life's sacred ways.

I grow new within, twirl round about,
Do-si-do with uncertainty,
make circles, shake away the broken
with new healing rhythms and rhymes spoken.

Out of "Great Everywhere,"
In thin Katahdin air
You sent Crow.

Abuse chains snapped!
Crow invites the "Good-bye dance"
as he offered the "Hello" greeting.
With Mother Nature, Crow
waves a feather over my Soul,

reminds me to know:

I don't "dance" alone.

87

Final Denia--Blue Blaze

I.
I look into a blue blaze,
calloused knothole,
see how unchecked, human pain
seeks horizons beyond horizons
of seven circling generations.
I dance this "good-bye" story
to stop horror,
end sexual abuse trauma.

"All Life is Sacred."
From its heart-wood core
new life is nourished.
Sapwood shadows,
grow sacred healing rings.
Embrace deep wounds.
Beauty smiles, leaves sing,
heal sexual abuse trauma.

Laser light strikes!
Out comes Sun,
spreading unexpected brightness!

I listen, see what I hear.
Trust shadow's healing
the world within.

II.
I dance grief back to blue blazes in Denia
away from this AT "writing" path.
Unsure of direction, I ask:
"is North this way or that?"

The answer arrives:
Trust the trees,
blue blaze, white blaze, the path.
I listen, hear what I see.
Grief is released,
puts me on my knees.

III.
I see two aged neighbors walk down the street.
His upper body bends as if to pray,
ask God, to lessen his pain.
He has "sticks" in each hand.
She stumbles along side,
has no place to hide.
Her "sticks" stabilizes her stride.

He sings a love song mostly on key
to his wobbly, stroke inflicted wife.
She smiles, hums, barely audible sounds.
Together, they shuffle along.

Bent, broken,
Alive and well.
Oh, so sweet.

IV
Glory Glistens!
The Dance ends.
Goodbye-Hello,
Life, Death, Life are one.

The story is done.

(Dedicated to Denia neighbors Hans and Doris Pietsch)

88

Black, White, Blue Blaze

The White-winged Angel
flaps her wings above the coffee bar.
Invited in, Pilar and I sit on stools like stars.

My old faded Crow Black fleece
Hangs like wings by the door.

I look at each:
White Angel, Crow Black AT Fleece.
Gratitude pulses through my veins.
I thank God, Mother Nature,
for soul healing I've gained.

I put down my pen,
Make no more pen marks
in the cherry wood.
Lift fingers off computer keys,
Rest hands on knees.

Crow caws down by Hurricane brook,
Reminds me, Nature heals,
provides best medicine.

Grief remains in this ending.
Hiking, writing are done.
Wherever, whenever I die
remembrance and meaning forever fly.
Beginning, ending are one.
Sun slips under the clouds.
White-light surrounds the orange sun-ball.
I deeply breathe free.
I am not in charge.
I am at the bar
where humanity ends.
Angel and Fleece
tell me "mystery begins.

89

Sacred Dream Encounter

I dream a cavernous open space.
Travel with an instructor,
receive credentials.
His light illuminates vision,
as I wonder, wander
in great underground space.

An umbilical cord connects like a "Y"
to outer sky and inner worlds.
Many kinds of Earth scenes
flow into me.

Inner world wonder
enlivens outer world appreciation.
A Doe appears.
I watch her watch me watch her.
Our sacred encounter heals.

90

White Blazes and God

I.
As it was on the AT, so it is today:
One can never expect what will happen
along a journey's way.
Am I walking the trail? Is the trail walking me?

An outer world trail
of blisters, bumps, rivers, trees
walks me.
The inner trail of, inner experience, healing
unfold meaning, offer hope.
I will reclaim my destiny.
The question is answered!

II.
A white blaze appears
a mile from John's house.
Eighteen more days of blazes
in Grand Cathedral's forest.
Eighteen more days of friendship,
celebration to feel your Spirit,
enjoy Your breath of life,

make it my own.

I head down the trail to complete the next section.
Open fields, soft hills, hardwood forests
hold waterfalls, rivulets, streams
in Housatonic River valley's morning steam.
Bird sounds, soft winds,
a Crow call or two pay tribute to You
for music, beauty, gratitude
given in dreams the way river banks shape streams;
It's a good time to walk, meditate, integrate
meaning of Crow feathers, friendship, inspiration, grace.

91

Epilogue: Finish

I.
I glide into another world.
Engines hum,
calm my melancholy soul.a
Silver bird flies
along Atlantic's cost
North toward Boston

I look West out the window.
Appalachian ridgeline,
punctuates the horizon
like a dragon's spine;
elicits sad, joyful tears.
of the last nine years.

That ridgeline holds my AT story.
I'm Finished!
Melancholy? Yes.
I soar in glory!

I crossed those summits,
dipped into dark, deep valleys,

fell to Earth in laughter,
left behind rivers of tears,
made wild with pain.
Lament unfulfilled expectations,
stifled by too much rain.

Swimming holes restore my soul,
Expose, wash away
old hidden pain;
replace it with jubilation, good cheer
and a found can of beer!

Nine years 2,190 miles,
One step at a time,
are left behind.
Big and small stories of
devastation, inspiration, healing
are in friendship shared.
What's done is done;
what needs to be said is said.

When healing happens,
some debris **IS** left behind.
Time now calls for celebration!

II.
From my seat I slide slow
through the window onto Crow's back,
take reins gifted by Black Horse.
Tuck in among soft Crow feathers.
I'm secure, safe, jubilant beyond measure.
Warm, blanketed with hope!
Oh! Such a treasure!

Thundah is here,
out there laughing, crying,
hoping, praying to finish next year.
Crow's never-ending presence
heals, protects, guides testimony,
tells him not to fear.

From sky belly rolls of mystery
above over Katahdin's Knife edge,
to "seeing" Crow
sit on a log in Georgia,
these memories greet me.

On Knife Edge I danced "hello";
I dance "goodbyes"
up here in the sky.

III.
We slip through clouds of puffy white
to the cherry plank desk top on which I write.
Long ago impressions left in wood
By pencil and pen
point beyond my ken
toward unfolding destiny.

One thing is for sure.
I didn't die in Denia!
I live alive in mystery!
For that, there is no death penalty!

About the Author

Rev. Dr. Gary E. Wehrwein is a retired ordained United Church of Christ minister. He lives in Keene, NH and Denia, Spain with his wife, Pilar. Their family is blended. Some family live in other parts of the world.

Gary is a former pastor of rural churches in VT and NH. His doctoral training led him to become a Licensed Clinical Pastoral Psychotherapist with Maps Counseling Service. There, he served as Clinical Director. His professional service included Hospice Chaplaincy, Community Counselor at a life-care center, and various consultancies with area churches.

Gary cares for and restores land. Stone wall building and restoration, brush clearing, selective tree thinning, bringing back over-grown fields, and a blueberry patch. Making new spaces for new gardens is part of his commitment to caring for the earth on which he lives.

Wehrwein now writes poetry.

Gary and Pilar have hiked many New England trails including all NH 4000' footers. The Camino de Santiago in Spain, Camino de Inca in Peru, and other trails in North and South America are on their "finished" list.

Notes

Denia is a Spanish port city on the Eastern Mediterranean coast where Gary E. Wehrwein and M. Pilar Abaurrea have a home.

The Appalachian Trail, or AT, is a 2,190-mile hiking trail from Baxter Peak (Mount Katahdin) in Maine to Springer Mountain in Georgia.

Mount Katahdin is an indigenous Penobscot name that means "Greatest Mountain."

Sturgeon is the most endangered fish species. Kennebec River pollution eliminated the Atlantic Sturgeon's spawning run for many years. In the 1990s, sturgeon again began swimming up the Kennebec River. Sturgeon spawn annually in Cobbessee Stream, a critical Kennebec River tributary That runs through downtown Gardiner, close behind the Accessory Shop, my parents' store.

Pamola Peak is the indigenous Penobscot language. It is a sub-peak of Mt. Katahdin. Pamola means "Wandering Bird spirit with human body."

Abraham is from the Biblical story of Abraham and Isaac, which is found in Genesis 22.

Yahweh is the Hebrew name for God.

Poseidon is a Greek mythical figure who presides over the sea and storms.

Baxter Peak is Mt. Katahdin's primary summit.

Pedophilia is a psychiatric disorder in which an adult has sexual fantasies about or engages in sexual acts with a prepubescent child.

Knife Edge is a narrow, dangerous, "knife-like" trail section that connects Pamola Peak with the summit of Baxter Peak, 5,267 feet away.

Crow is the most intelligent bird found worldwide. Crows symbolize new beginnings, joy, freedom, darkness, shadow, and death. Crows are tricksters.

AT trail shelters are backcountry overnight sleeping places that give hikers protection against bad weather and provide overnight sleeping.

The Zip Stove is a small, light backpacking cook stove. It is easy to carry, burns almost anything, and cooks hot and fast.

Golden Road is a prominent logging road from the Maine Wilderness to Canada.

Shadow represents those elements, energies, and agendas in us or our affiliative associations that contradict our professed values when brought to consciousness. The Shadow is not evil, per se, though much evil derives from it; instead, Shadow embodies the contrarian dimensions of our souls. What is wrong in the world is deficient in us as well. (James Hollis, *Living Between Worlds*).

Trail names are unique nicknames given to long-distance hikers. They don't look for trail names; Trail names come to the hiker.

Trail Blaze is a two-by-six splash of white, blue, yellow, and sometimes red paint markings on the AT. White blazes, usually seen on trees and stones, mark the main AT trail—blue marks unique side trails, alternative routes, shelter placement, time outs for injury, etc. Blue blazes provide secondary information about anything related to a hiker's AT journey.

Agiocochook is an indigenous name for Mount Washington, the mountain home of the Great Spirit, the Giant One.

Kancamagus is a road through the White Mountains connecting N. Conway, NH Highway and Lincoln, N.H.

John Garvan is a now-deceased, long-time, kind, generous friend, musician, and occasional hiking companion.

The Weight of Generations reflects the truth that unless confronted, the "sins" of mothers and fathers live on to seven generations.

Kancamagus Highway runs through the White Mountains, connecting N. Conway and Lincoln, New Hampshire.

Aria Wehrwein is my granddaughter.

"Ultreia" is the Spanish word for "forward!"

Troya is a small "Mom and Pop" store near our Denia *"adosado"*.

AT-LT Junction is a Vermont trail junction of the Appalachian Trail and Long Trail.

Mt. Greylock is a Veterans WW II Memorial Monument Plaque Monument.

"Adosado" is a Spanish word for attached row houses.

"**All Life is Sacred**" is the title of the first sermon I preached on 10/15/1966 in the Second Congregational Church, United Church of Christ, Londonderry, Vermont. This affirmation is a core belief.

Rebecca's "Inn" refers to a Pastoral Counselor, Colleague, and friend of Laughin Thundah and Crow Feathah. She lives in New Jersey near the AT.

Limmers are high-quality hiking boots that continue to serve me well.

Kirkridge Retreat is a popular retreat center located on Kittantinny Ridge.

Half Way is at Pine Grove Furnace, PA—central rest and resupply stop.

Trail Magic refers to an unexpected, magical, synchronistic, ineffable experience and/or circumstance that calls attention to matters of mystery hiking the Appalachian Trail.

A Trail Angel is a person who provides an AT hiker with an unexpected gift, including food, beer, wine, feathers of meaning, encouragement, a "Ride to town," etc.

At times, Laughing Thundah, Stick, and I called ourselves "**Trinity**".

Pilar through the AT Journal, where I placed an Ad in the personals section. The Ad said, "I cook with garlic and ginger." This became the "catch". "So do I," she said. We are husband and wife.

AT Plaque On Springer Mountain Summit, a plaque is bolted into stone. In 1934, the Georgia Appalachian Mountain Trail Club established: "The Appalachian Trail is a footpath for those who seek fellowship with the Wilderness."

Hans and Dorothia Pietsch, our friendly Denia neighbors, live two *adosados* from us.

The Dream features a white-winged angel, a black fleece I used for most of my journey, and a blue blaze to indicate the critical significance of the dream.

Acknowledgments

Writing about the trail requires many more miles than the 2100+ that comprise the AT, with so many kind people to thank for helping me along the way. I could never hope to acknowledge all those who have provided me with their encouragement and support. For simplicity's sake I would like to thank my editor, Conrad Kanagy, who affirmed the value of this work and prodded me to push through. His writers' group collective continues to be a valuable learning and healing tool for me. I thank David Reynolds for his stedfast friendship and for lending a keen listening ear while walking me through the confusion of Jungian psychology. I am deeply indebted to Bill Beardslee for the many generous hours of conversation about writing poetry. He gave me the "inspirational boot" to write first lines that connected me with other resources. Last in line but first in importance I extend my sincere gratitude to my sons and their families and in particular I want to thank my loving wife, Pilar, for many years of encouragement, care, on-going affection, technical support and never-ending patience when I lost my way.